BOSCH

BOSCH

Robert L. Delevoy

SKIRA

RIZZOLI
NEW YORK

Cover illustration:
The Adoration of the Magi: Crystal Globe and Bird,
detail of the central panel, about 1510.

First published 1960
First paperback edition 1990

Published in the United States of America in 1990 by
Rizzoli INTERNATIONAL PUBLICATIONS, INC.
300 Park Avenue South/New York 10010

© 1990 by Editions d'Art Albert Skira S.A., Geneva
Translated from the French by Stuart Gilbert
89 Route de Chêne
1208 Geneva, Switzerland

Library of Congress Cataloging-in-Publication Data

Delevoy, Robert L.
  [Bosch. English]
  Bosch: a biographical and critical study/by Robert L. Delevoy;
  translated by Stuart Gilbert.
     p.   cm.
  Translation of: Bosch.
  Includes bibliographical references and index.
  ISBN 0-8478-1348-7
  1. Bosch, Hieronymus, d. 1516.   2. Painters-Netherlands-
  Biography.   I. Bosch, Hieronymus, d. 1516.   II. Title.
ND653.B65D353   1991
759.9492–dc20   90-50885
                                                        CIP

CONTENTS

THE LIFE OF BOSCH

A PROVINCIAL CAREER

It is in the shadows that momentous
encounters take place.

ALFRED FABRE-LUCE

O N mid-summer's day of the year 1520, after a long ride on a
sluggish Brabantine horse in driving rain, Dürer arrived at the
gate of 's Hertogenbosch—he was by now in the worst of
tempers—and was welcomed by a group of local goldsmiths, of whom
he says no more in his diary than that they received him with much
civility. It was a "pretty town," he noticed, with some "fine churches,"
but he expressed no surprise at finding, in a region where brick-build-
ings were the rule, an enormous stone cathedral which had just been
finished in the now declining Late Gothic style. Of Hieronymus Bosch,
who had died there only a few years before, he said not a word!

Did he deliberately omit mention of a painter whose art he
regarded with contemptuous indifference? Quite likely, concerned as
he was with the new values rich in promise for the future now in the
ascendant. With his passion for measurement and mathematics, for
science and geometry, Dürer must have felt nothing but disdain for a
master who, in his eyes, embodied the defunct traditions of a bygone
age. For it is impossible to believe he was unacquainted with Bosch's

work. Dürer had visited the palace of Marguerite of Austria, at Malines, where two pictures by Bosch were to be seen: A *Temptation of St Anthony* and a *Judgment of God*. The latter had been painted in 1504 for the "very noble pleasure" of Philip the Fair by "Jheronimus van Aeken, styled Bosch, of Bois-le-Duc, to whom thirty-six livres were paid" (Register F. 190, *Archives du Département du Nord*, Lille).

At that time, 's Hertogenbosch (the original Dutch name of Bois-le-Duc), "lying two leagues off the river Meuse and twelve leagues distant from Antwerp," was an important commercial center. It "held the fourth and final place among the four capital cities of Brabant." In his famous *Descrittione di tutti i Paesi Bassi* (1567) Ludovico Guicciardini notes that the town produced "much cloth and... an incalculable quantity of exceedingly well-tempered knives and vast numbers of pins." Populous, enterprising, "dowered with edifices pleasing to the eye," standing in wooded country at the confluence of the rivers Aa and Dommel, the town guarded the northern approaches of a province flanked by the Country of Flanders and the Principality of Liège. After forming part of the dominions of the Duke of Burgundy, it passed in 1477 to the House of Austria, through the marriage of Mary of Burgundy to Prince Maximilian, the Hapsburgs' heir. But isolated as it was in the depths of the North Brabantine countryside, far from the great political centers, Bois-le-Duc had ignored the march of progress and retained the customs, outlook, and traditional ways of life and thought of the Middle Ages. Far removed from the influences of Franco-Burgundian culture, nourished on folklore, passionately addicted to Mystery plays and delighted by the woodcuts illustrating the *Ars moriendi* (the most popular book in northern Europe in the late 15th and early 16th century), practical-minded yet superstitious, the citizens of Bois-le-Duc had greatly relished the Low Countries' version of *Tondale's Visions*, printed within their walls in 1484 by Gerardus Leempt, a newcomer from Nimeguen. On a superficial view, it seems almost incredible that this provincial backwater with its uneventful past and hidebound traditions can have been the birthplace of so singular, so dazzlingly original a painter. Nevertheless allowance must be made for the remarkable energy and activity of the local merchants and craftsmen; for a collective mentality which may well have fostered the emergence of a genius such as that of Bosch; and for the spectacular initiative of the inhabitants in building the church of St John to the designs of Alaert du Hameel, architect, mason, head of his guild, stone carver and, in his leisure hours, a superb copperplate engraver. One of the few men in Bois-le-Duc whose companionship Bosch may well have found congenial, du Hameel supervised the building of the church of St John from 1478 to 1494, during which time the south transept was finished and work on the nave began. Summoned to Louvain, where he held the post of city architect from 1495 to 1502, he was consulted in 1500 by the city of Antwerp in connection with the tower of Notre-Dame, which then was nearing completion and for which he is believed to have designed the spire. It is quite within the bounds of probability that Bosch went with him to Louvain and Antwerp; or else joined him there. Anyhow, du Hameel must have been for Bosch an invaluable source of information as to what was taking place in the outside world. What is more, in his capacity as an engraver he was the first to interpret his friend's paintings. Remarkable for their free and sensitive handling, his prints are extemely rare (only eleven subjects are known and most of them have come down to us in a single copy).

Both men were members of the Brotherhood of Our Lady (*Illustre Lieve-Vrouwe Broederschap*), and the archives of this association (account books and membership lists) have yielded the only documents that throw any light on Bosch's life, of which Carel van Mander, writing early in the 17th century, admitted that he knew nothing. These sources were first tapped in 1860 by the Belgian historian Alexandre Pinchart. In this century, they were systematically investigated by Jan Mosmans (1947), H. J. M. Ebeling (1948) and D. Bax (1949). Though no sensational discoveries were made, their research established a few points of fact sufficiently explicit to give us a fairly clear idea of the milieu in which Bosch's highly original genius ripened and bore fruit.

One of the points established beyond all doubt is that his social activities were for the most part concerned with the Brotherhood of Our Lady, which had adopted a swan as emblem on its coat-of-arms. He was admitted to membership in 1486 under the name of Jheronimus Anthonissoen van Aken (i.e. Hieronymus, son of Anthony, of Aachen). As custom required, he was tonsured and took to wearing the curious homespun garments adopted by members of the fraternity, a derivative of the costume worn by ecclesiastics. Less than two years later, in 1488, he was sworn in as a *frère-juré*, and thus promoted to the rank of "notable." He took part on this occasion—the first Monday after the first of January—in the annual Swan Banquet, so called because one or two roast swans invariably figured on the menu. In July of the same year Bosch himself played host to his colleagues at a dinner given in the half-timbered house he occupied in the center of the town, beside the triangular marketplace. His wife, Aleid van de Meervenne (born in 1453), was the orphaned daughter of well-to-do patrician parents; they were married about 1478. Herself a member of the fraternity since the age of sixteen, Aleid had inherited a country estate at Oirschot, a village about twenty miles from Bois-le-Duc.

The illustrious Brotherhood of Our Lady did a good deal more than organize prayer meetings for its members, preside over funeral ceremonies and distribute bread to the poor. One of its functions was to train the orchestra that performed in the cathedral, to which it also supplied ornaments, altarpieces and pictures. It had a theatrical company which specialized in staging dramatic performances of various kinds, Mystery plays, devil dances, ballets of ghosts and skeletons, farces and *diableries*, all of which called for a formidable array of stage properties: iron helmets, false noses (in leather), painted costumes, masks of cloth and hide, embroidered mantles, banners of silk or gold, tallow candles and oil torches. For obvious reasons plays and pageants of this nature had a strong appeal to a God-fearing (and Satan-fearing) people, ridden with superstitions and obsessed by atavistic phobias stemming from the Dark Ages. Typically Nordic counterparts of the

Medici carnivals and the humanist festivities of Florence, these performances savored of the medievalism lingering on the provincial milieu of a walled town effectively cut off from outside influences.

Playing as he did an active part in stage performances and religious ceremonies, Bosch must have ranked as a leading figure in this closed community, a higly respectable and highly respected citizen. The account books of the brotherhood (*Rekeningen van St Jan*) record, among other commissions, the fact that he was employed to paint coats of arms and to design a copper crown and model for a Crucifixion. It is here that we find his name mentioned for the first time: in 1480-1481 "Jeroen die maelre" supplied the "Lieve-Vrouwe Broederschap" with two wings of an altarpiece which his father, Antonius van Aken, had left unfinished at his death in about 1478-1479. This entry is enough to give us a general idea of his family background and training as a painter. Equally significant, in this context, is the fact that he had two uncles, Johannes and Thomas, who were also painters, and that his grandfather, too, who died in 1456, had followed the same profession. Tradition ascribes to the latter a fresco in the local cathedral, deriving morphologically from the Van Eycks; it represents *Christ on the Cross* and is dated 1444. Charles de Tolnay sees in this work the prototype of a *Crucifixion* (now in Brussels) which Bosch painted early in his career. The above-mentioned records also inform us that in 1493-1494 Bosch supplied the master glassworkers Henricken Bueken and Willem Lombart with designs for several stained glass windows for the chapel of the brotherhood, the handsomest of the seven chapels of retreat in the choir of St John's church. The picture we get from these documents is that of a highly versatile artist, capable of turning an expert hand to many different crafts.

Early in the 17th century Bois-le-Duc was visited by the Flemish traveler and historian J. B. Gramaye, as keen an observer as Guicciardini. In a brief chronicle (*Taxandria*, 1610) he mentions having seen several pictures by Bosch in the local cathedral, notably an altarpiece whose outer wings, executed in 1489 (D. Bax, *Ontcijfering van J. Bosch*, 1949), represented *Abigail bowing down before David* and a triptych depicting the *Siege of Bethulia*, the *Murder of Holofernes*, the *Flight of the Assyrians, Mordecai and Esther*, and the *Triumph of the Jewish People*. These Biblical scenes were destroyed when the church was pillaged by fanatical Reformers in 1629. One work by Bosch had already been removed to a safe place: the *Adoration of the Magi*, bearing the coats of arms of the Brouckhorst and Bosschuyse families and signed in Gothic characters. It hung originally in the chapel of the Brotherhood of Our Lady. No doubt because it was a finer, more attractive work than the others, it had been deposited in the Town Hall after barely escaping destruction in an initial outbreak of iconoclasm on August 22, 1566. A few months later it found its way to Brussels, to the house of Jean de Casembroot, Lord of Backerseele, "near the Couwenberghe gate." There it was seized and confiscated on April 14, 1567, by the agents of Philip II, who had it placed in the Escorial in 1574 (A. Pinchart, *Archives des Arts*, Ghent, 1860). One of the proudest possessions of the Prado (since 1839), it is probably the most carefully finished work ever painted by Bosch.

Alongside his activities on behalf of the brotherhood to which he belonged, Bosch must have produced a considerable body of painting in his small studio on the marketplace. For whom? For himself first of all, certainly (whatever other students of Bosch may think and say). He had so many dreams to give form and substance to, so rich an inner life to body forth, so many delectable liberties to take. Rare indeed were such ambitions, personal to a degree, in an age when, as a general rule, paintings were still made to order. Yet his work achieved success from the very start. Through what channels did these visions of a *terra incognita* explored by him alone come to the notice of the world at large? How was it that the name of Bosch became so well known in the courts of Europe, while he himself seems never to have crossed the frontiers of his native province? One wonders whether Erasmus may not have been his ambassador abroad. In spite of his extreme youth (he was barely seventeen), the future author of the *Praise of Folly* was already a man of ripe understanding, as Johannes Agricola tells us, when he came to Bois-le-Duc to complete his education at the school of the Brothers of the Common Life. There he must have seen Bosch's work and been much impressed by it. Possibly it was this meeting with Bosch that gave the young Desiderarius Erasmus the idea of dabbling in colors himself, and led him to quarrel over the matter with his narrow-minded guardians, who were determined he should follow a monastic career. But this desire to be an artist persisted even after he had moved from Bois-le-Duc to the monastery of Steyn, where he was dispensed from attending evening services so as to be free to paint in the leisure moments thus provided. Unfortunately no trace of these nocturnal activities has survived. Should any sketches or paintings by Erasmus' hand ever be discovered, it would come as no surprise to find them marked by the eerie fancies we associate with Bosch.

In the very year that Thomas More's *Utopia* was published, Bosch passed away, leaving, it seems, no children. A funeral ceremony of great pomp was held in the chapel of the Brotherhood of Our Lady on August 9, 1516. The entry of his death in the register entitled "Nomina decanorum et praepositorum" reads as follows:

> Obitus fratrum A° 1516: Hieronimus Aquen, als Bosch, insignis pictor.

Another ledger records his death in these terms:

> Hieronymus Aquens, alias Bosch seer vermaerd schilder, Obiit 1516.

These two documents prove that Bosch was a painter highly esteemed in his own lifetime. His age in 1516, the year of his death, is a moot question. Sixty-five would seem to be a reasonable estimate. In that case he was born at Bois-le-Duc (where his family is mentioned as early as the mid-13th century) about 1450, at the time, that is to say, when Rogier van der Weyden had reached the climatic point of his career. He was an almost exact contemporary of Leonardo da Vinci —who was equally far from being "a kind of incomplete and startling genius unrelated to his period."

Apart from the very meager information that can be gleaned from the archives of his native town, it must be confessed that sadly little is known of Bosch's personal life. We know that he belonged to the well-to-do class. We know that he was a prominent member of a lay brotherhood, but one of the strictest Christian principles. But as regards his way of life, the kind of man he was, we are left in the dark. Not that we greatly care to know whether he led a life of blameless domesticity or otherwise. The knowledge that Goya was a lady-killer, Perugino a criminal and Duccio something of a tippler has no bearing on the pleasure we get from contemplating their works. Yet the very uniqueness, the peculiar bias of his art, piques our curiosity and it is hard to refrain from wondering what prompted him to paint in the way he did, and what, if any, were his sources.

Can we make a reasonable conjecture as to the nature of his intellectual background? What illuminated manuscripts, incunabula, or printed books may have come his way? What woodcuts, copperplate engravings, or color sheets might he have seen, borrowed or collected? What contemporary paintings, or paintings of the recent past, might he have set eyes on? What exactly was his attitude toward religion? What were his relations with the Carthusians of Bois-le-Duc and the Brothers of the Common Life? Did he frequent the circle of the Gnostics and lead, as it were, a double life? Did he belong to some heretical sect? Did he haunt the laboratory of some adept of the alchemist Nicolas Flamel? Did he dabble in black magic? What were his real views regarding witchcraft? Did he find sadistic pleasure in observing the effects of torture? Did he indulge in the perversions of a licentious age, or did he bring to bear on them the reproving eye of a moralist? Was he a true mystic or simply a daydreamer? What part did he play in the busy, industrious life of his fellow citizens?

There is no question that the "case" of Bosch is hard to diagnose. Tact, circumspection and objectivity are needed for an understanding of the mental processes of this great artist. We have to feel our way, step by cautious step. No direct method of approach is possible as it is with Goya, Rubens, or Michelangelo. True, we cannot see him otherwise than with present-day eyes: we read into him our own dreams, our contemporary anxieties and misgivings, our yearnings to escape from life's realities, for somehow these seem to coincide with the unique "message" of his art. This no doubt is why it answers in a very special way to our modern sensibility. Yet, no sooner do we set to analysing his works, than they elude our grasp, we cease to *see* them; they dazzle us and we forget that after all Bosch was, first and foremost, a painter. To hail him as "the first modern painter," however, as so many have done, is certainly a mistake. For it involves playing fast and loose with the facts of history, and placing him in a false perspective of time and space. It is the sense of bafflement we feel when gazing at his pictures that gives rise to the questions, seasonable or unseasonable, which we voiced above and which rise to our minds almost instinctively today, but which, for the most part, would have been quite unthinkable in the Late Middle Ages. We ask irrelevant or misleading questions because our angle of vision does not tally with that of the age we are seeking to elucidate. These questions have no bearing on the 15th century; they are anachronisms, colored by the laws, conventions, prejudices and habits of thought of modern man. We are far too ready to forget that our own standards cannot provide a yardstick for our estimates of a bygone age and its *Weltanschauung*.

The mentality of pre-Renaissance man was infinitely fresher, freer, less sophisticated and less disciplined than ours. So many things that nowadays appear disgusting, licentious or degrading were not so to him; to him they were an integral part of daily life and added zest to it. In our churches the congregation observes the strictest decorum, and so does the preacher in his sermon. But the churches of Bosch's day resounded with sensuous, outspoken sermons, teeming with voluptuous imagery which would shock and horrify present-day Christians. Women attended church service in low-necked gowns and gossiped with one another during the service. Prostitutes came and went, openly seeking customers (Huizinga, *The Waning of the Middle Ages*, London

1924). The church was a place of rendez-vous, and it was quite usual for a woman to get up in the middle of the service and step across the aisle to greet with a kiss her lover, just arrived, "while the priest was consecrating the host and the people worshiping." Bawdy pictures were hawked in the portals, and even in the church itself lewdness and licence were frankly tolerated. The great religious processions were equally indecorous, and for many who took part in them, pilgrimages were occasions not so much for fulfilling a pious vow as for gratifying sinful appetites more easily. It has been aptly observed that "only a social order steeped in religious sentiment and taking faith for granted indulges in such excesses." Moreover, we are too apt to forget that alchemy was accepted in those days as a perfectly legitimate means of access to the supramundane, and its adepts, far from being hostile to the church, were often better Christians than many of the monks. "Alchemy came under suspicion only when it lapsed into magic, or when it served to propagate heretical doctrines" (Caron and Hutin, *Les Alchimistes*, Paris 1959). But the fact must not be overlooked that alchemy had now come to be the prerogative of a swarm of charlatans whose public performances exploited the credulity of the masses, and sowed the seeds of doubt from which there sprang so many sects of heretics, so many practitioners of black magic and witchcraft. The frontier between faith and superstition was blurred or broken down. The Church did what it could. It anathematized both witches and magicians as arch-heretics and armed its inquisitors with a convenient manual, the famous *Malleus Maleficarum*, the "Hammer of Witches." It issued the no less famous bull *Summis desiderantes affectibus*, a scathing indictment of the wave of superstition that was undermining its authority. But the movement was too strong and the contagion too widespread; men's minds teemed with wild, irrational fancies whose mysterious power could be curbed by reason only. But the currents of modern thought had not yet filtered into this provincial backwater: Bosch still could take for granted the imperiled values to which the men around him still clung with the old fervor. Placed at the crossroads of two ages, he illustrates a conflict of ideas, emotions and tastes. Torn between hope and dark foreboding, between faith and doubt, his œuvre may justly be regarded as a sign of the times both fascinating and instructive. It sublimates the rantings and extravagances of the popular preachers on to the plane of art. To the writings of the age it adds eye-filling plastic equivalents and gives to proverbs pungent forms. Unaffected by the new forces soon to shatter the structure of medieval thought, it reveals the mores of that intriguing age in vivid imagery and endows abstractions with a compelling actuality.

There is no knowing which of the extant works was earliest. Bosch's œuvre has come down to us in scattered fragments, the jetsam of successive waves of iconoclasm. Of the thirty panels or so which can be safely ascribed to him, only seven bear his signature: *The Hay Wagon* (Madrid), *St John in Patmos* (Berlin), a *Temptation of St Anthony* (Lisbon), an *Adoration of the Magi* (Madrid), *St Christopher* (Rotterdam), the *Altarpiece of St Julia* and the *Altarpiece of the Hermits* (both in the Ducal Palace, Venice). Varying as is their quality and strongly marked as are their differences, any attempt to determine their chronological order is a hopeless, unrewarding task. Such is their originality that no clues are forthcoming as to the possible influence of better known contemporary artist. Costumes are handled so freely and fancifully that no particular fashion can be singled out for purposes of dating. Only the vaguest of *ante* or *postquam* timings can be inferred from their formal developments, which in the case of so many other painter's œuvres make it possible to trace the evolution of an artist's style within the frame of reference of a coherent plastic system (spacial construction, definition of volume, compositional structure, and so forth). There is no common denominator between the evolution of Bosch's art and that of contemporary painters. His is a world apart, self-sufficient, indivisible. Analysis of his art, however close, leads nowhere. The utmost we can hope is to detect some fleeting sequence of intentions hidden in its depths and fluctuations.

The Seven Deadly Sins, about 1475.

THE PHASE OF DOUBT

A CRITICAL REFLECTION

> Man lives and moves in what he sees;
> but he sees only what he dreams.
>
> PAUL VALÉRY

JUST after his marriage, Bosch, it seems, moved out to the country village of Oirschot, where, through his wife, he had inherited a house and land. Apparently it was during his stay there that he painted his earliest works, or at any rate the one that for us undoubtedly marks the beginning of his career: a table top (*tabla*) representing the *Seven Deadly Sins* (Prado, Madrid). Even after nearly five centuries, some features of the village of Oirschot are recognizable in the setting of the scenes. Very unusual for the time (though logical enough in this instance) is the fact that the composition is intended to be seen from above, i.e. from a high angle of vision. It contains four circular medallions, one at each corner, representing the four Last Things: *Death*, *The Last Judgment*, *Paradise* and *Hell*. These are darker and look older than the large central tondo; indeed they appear to be by a different hand. The tondo is painted in a bright scale of pinks, blues, ochres and greens, as fresh as if they had been laid in yesterday. The center of the panel represents the eye of God, its pupil fringed with rays of light (Fraenger counts 128 of these, and interprets them as evidence

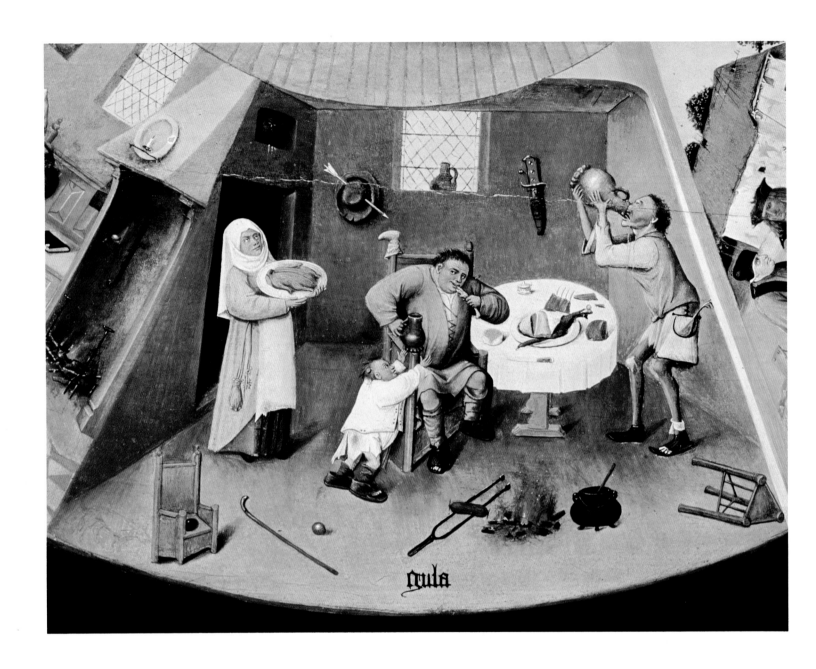

that Bosch belonged to a sect of heretics). Under the pupil are the words *Cave, cave, Deus videt* (Beware, beware, God sees thee); the inscription reinforces the pictorial warning addressed to hardened sinners who have lost all sense of being watched by God. We see them indulging their evil propensities in seven "mansions" grouped around the central eye and forming a circular composition divided into segments. Each is like a very slightly enlarged Gothic miniature and converts the allegory into a genre scene. Vanity, Anger, Lust, Sloth, Gluttony, Covetousness and Envy supply the pretexts for a picture sequence of incidents of daily life viewed by a mocking, ironical, critical eye. With this *tabla* Bosch ushered in the painting of "realistic" scenes used as vehicles for a social message and a moral lesson. Moreover, the work as a whole is ingeniously contrived to suggest the idea of a ball, a sphere, a globe: the terrestrial globe, *imago mundi*, microcosm of the universe. From now on the image of a sphere recurs like an obsession in the work of this great visionary; and a cosmic referent will always be found to underlie the moral purport of each picture.

The Seven Deadly Sins, about 1475. Segments:

◁ Gluttony

▷ Vanity

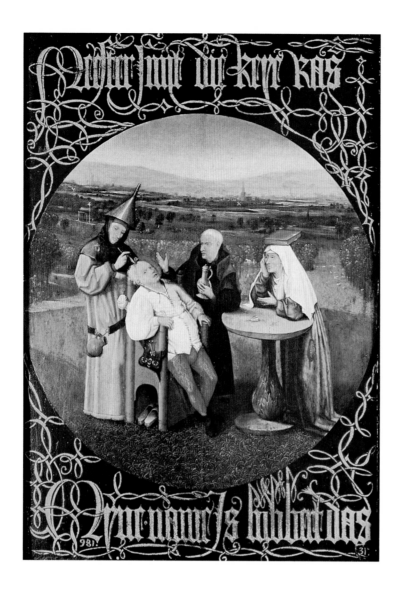

The Cure of Folly,
1475-1480.

The *Cure of Folly* (Prado, Madrid) is in the same vein. The simple, elementary composition, the sketchy modeling of figures, the broken folds of costumes, and the unsure geometry of the accessories make it clear this is an early work. The execution oscillates between the decorative, detailed calligraphy of the foreground and the tonal modulation pervading the rest of the scene. Three adroitly echeloned registers (ochre, green and blue) suggest spatial recession. This is an innovation of capital importance. It inaugurates the far-flung panoramic background without figures, rendered in purely painterly terms, that is to say in terms of gradations of tone producing the illusion of depth and space. And here again, as in the *Seven Sins*, this tendency to generalization has its symbolic counterpart in the circular (*tondo*) structure of the picture. Both the shape and overall arrangement emphasize the general purport, didactic and moral, of the scene represented, which fits into its spatial context far more smoothly than is commonly realized by beholders who fail to observe the subtle cohesion of the mauves, blue-grays, whites, browns, purplish reds and vermilions of the costumes, harmonizing so well with the basic tonalities of the background against which they stand out.

A rhyming inscription describes the scene, which had its origin in Netherlandish literature and popular imagery:

> Meester snijt die keie ras
> Mijne name is Lubbert Das.
>
> Master, hurry up and cut the stone out
> My name is Lubbert Das.

Bosch puts this unwise request in the mouth of a plump old man whom he christens Lubbert (i.e. lubber), a name that turns up frequently in Flemish literature and always signifies a fool or simpleton. The "master" appealed to is of course a dangerous charlatan. Taking advantage of his patient's credulity, and armed with a surgical knife, he is about to carry into execution a popular saying: *iemand van de kei snijden*, to cut someone's "stone" (out of his skull), in other words to cure him of his folly. According to Bax, the word *kei* probably derives from *Keye*, the name of an uncouth knight of the Round Table. The healer either cures the patient or makes him even madder than before. Obviously it is the latter result that is to be expected here: the "doctor" is a trickster. Instead of a hat he wears a funnel, symbol of deception (in the 16th century, by extension, the funnel became an emblem of infidelity). A monk encourages the guileless victim with an unctuous gesture while a nun watches the operation with bland unconcern. A closed book (a Bible, a medical treatise or a *volumen*?) is placed on her head. The wheel and gibbet in the background symbolize moral degradation and generalize the indictment of human folly and perversity implicit in the scene, which brings to mind some lines on the same theme by the Flemish poet Jan van Stijevoort. Though written several decades later (1524), they relate to the same tradition, racy of the soil, as that of the *Cure of Folly*:

> Die keye verborghen sal bat gedijen
> dan bloot gelijk die rape moet
> want waerhy bloot men souden wt snijen
> en waer hij wte ten waer niet goet
> want half sot half vroet wel leuen doet.

> The hidden stone ripens fast
> Then laid bare like a turnip
> Can easily be cut out at last.
> But even then the danger isn't past.
> That man lives best who's fain to live half mad, half sane.

The Conjurer in the Municipal Museum of Saint-Germain-en-Laye, not far from Paris, always comes as a surprise, however often one sets eyes on it. The reason is that, though so small a picture (53 × 65 cm), it produces so remarkable an impression of monumentality. This effect is due to the compelling synthesis of local tones, to the proportions of the figures and to their graduated disposition against a neutral ground (a decrepit brown-brick wall under a dark sea-green sky). Van Mander aptly observes that, in the draping of his figures, Bosch "departs quite noticeably from the old system, which consisted in multiplying the creases and sharp edges of garments; his treatment of them is broad and firm, and he often painted *alla prima*, which has not prevented his works from remaining very fine."

Despite an obvious attempt to render the central motif—i.e. the table—in perspective, the scene is unrelated to measurable space and the layout is determined wholly by its topological content. Hence the sharply defined profiles, the two-dimensional bodies, the schematic gestures, the gross, bloated faces. Here Bosch has epitomized the crowd, summed up the human condition in this group of feckless men and women watching with rapt attention the conjurer's performance.

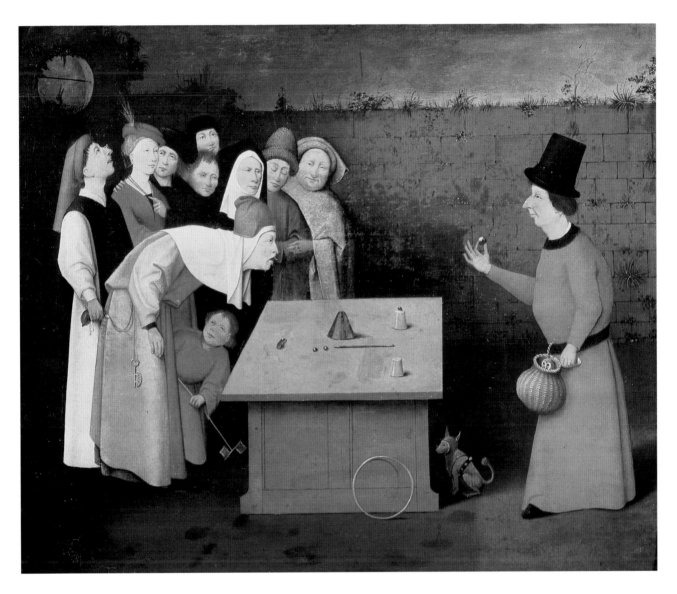

The Conjurer, 1475-1480.

These brilliantly diversified, wonderfully lifelike figures, for all their seeming realism, stem from the same subjective sources as those of the *Seven Deadly Sins* and the *Cure of Folly*, and are located in the same psychological context, the same moral desert. Certain details disclose the meaning of this little masterpiece, whose style, technique and color-scheme justify us in regarding it as an original work by the hand of Bosch himself, though some have seen in it only a well-executed copy. Sitting on its haunches behind the table, concealed from the onlookers, is a small monkey wearing a fool's cap. A frog (symbol of credulity) has just dropped on the table from the gaping mouth of a guileless clodhopper who, bent double, is spellbound by the old trick of the strolling thimblerigger. The little ball, deftly twirled between the conjurer's practiced fingers, is about to vanish, and so is the simpleton's purse, to the great joy of the little boy beside him: it is already in the hands of the conjurer's confederate, a well-dressed bystander who is obviously trying to look as innocent and unconcerned as possible. "He who lets himself be fooled by conjuring tricks," says the Flemish proverb, "loses his money and becomes the laughingstock of children." True, but a similar lack of discernment, the same witlessness and credulity, too often lead to heresy—symbolized by the owl, here seen peeping out of a wicker gamebag hanging from the conjurer's belt.

The general laxity of morals and the corruption of the clergy had begun to assume alarming proportions. We have already seen a nun watching the removal of the "stone of folly"; another has slipped into the curiously assorted crowd watching the conjurer. And now, under a pink oriflamme with the devil's emblem on it (the crescent), we find a nun and a monk playing leading parts in the *Ship of Fools* (Louvre, Paris). On the board between them, which does duty for a table, is a dish of cherries (symbol of sensual pleasure). Surrounded by a shipload of grotesque characters plainly the worse for drink, they sit face to face, singing lustily to the sound of a lute (which at that time had erotic associations), eager to snatch a bite of the cake dangling in front of their noses. In the background, perched on a slender broken branch attached to the boat, and recognizable by his cap with ass's ears, his bauble, and the mockhead dangling above his shoulders, a professional fool is drinking from a bowl of some heady liquor. This figure, painted *con brio* in olive green picked out with little dabs of white, tells out against the dark green foliage of a hazel tree (symbol, in 16th-century literature, of stupidity). A man, brandishing a knife (sexual symbol or

The Ship of Fools, about 1490.

The Ship of Fools. Drawing.

Death and the Miser. Drawing.

emblem of anger?) is climbing the mast, so as to cut down a roast chicken attached to it. Again an owl keeps watch on the proceedings, this time from a mass of leafage at the masthead.

Obviously nothing has been left to chance in this panel, all that now remains of a lost triptych. Transposed into an imaginary space, everything, down to the least detail, is oriented toward the proclamation of dramatic, pessimistic, unpalatable truths. On a superficial view this picture may seem merely anecdotal, a burlesque piece cluttered up with more or less amusing details. But if we study it more closely and situate it in its temporal context, the symbols here employed regain something of the significance they had at the time when the picture was painted. The levels of meaning it conceals are too numerous and varied for it to be an easy picture to interpret. Nor should any one meaning be emphasized at the expense of others. The ship is, as it were, a symbiosis. Its fragile hull rests, precariously swaying, on the surface of a dark green sea (dark-green being the hue of moral degradation). It is at once the ancient symbol of the Church, a refuge of the outcasts of society (an idea widely current in medieval Europe), and the emblem of a free-and-easy local club named the *Blau Schuyt* (the Blue Boat). The ship, moreover, was a favorite leitmotiv of didactic literature from the 14th century on. It was Paul Lafond who in 1914 first pointed out another possible source of this picture: the *Narrenschiff*, a famous satirical poem written in the vernacular by the Alsatian humanist Sebastian Brant and published in Basel in 1494. Translated a few years later into French by Rivière (*La Nef des Fous*, Paris 1497) and into Latin by Jakob Locher (*Navis Stultifera*, Basel 1497), it was reissued by the scholarly Flemish printer Judocus Badius Ascensius, who published it in Paris in 1501 under the title *Stultiferae Naves*. Among the woodcuts illustrating this edition is one showing a boat laden with six drunken fools. It is far from certain, however, that Bosch's picture was painted *after* the publication of Brant's *Narrenschiff*. Indeed, despite its many high qualities, its execution seems to us too coarse to admit of any date later than 1490.

The Hay Wagon, about 1490:
An Episode of the Struggle for Life *and* The Team of Demons, *details of the central panel.*

The *Hay Wagon* (Prado, Madrid; copy in the Escorial) was probably painted at about the same time. For the disparity between the moral scope of the work and the relative poorness of the *facture* (even allowing for the ravages of time) suggests an early date. Richly diverse as is the color-scheme, there is a textural dryness and skimpiness, and a certain clumsiness of execution. Outlines are blurred and figures show no signs as yet of the plastic mastery we find in such finely wrought works as the *Adoration of the Magi* (Prado) and the *Garden of Earthly Delights* (Prado).

The Hay Wagon:
The Original Sin *and* The Exile to Hell, *left and right panel.*

Technically speaking, the *Hay Wagon* is the least accomplished of the series of great triptychs. Yet we cannot but recognize the compelling sweep and power of this vast synthesis of the multifarious, sometimes conflicting data of a remarkably wide experience of life on several planes. Bosch's first large-scale encyclopedic painting, figuring forth the wide world as a microcosm (a type of picture which was frequent

The Hay Wagon, central panel.

in the early 15th century but soon went out of fashion), is a creation of a restless, pessimistic mind, of searching, yet imprecise thought. With its curious intermingling of both reality and dream, it illustrates the mental unrest of the age, an age of such unbridled license that the distinctions between man and beast seemed to be fading out. Man had gone astray and lost touch with his mission. Bosch sought to define the human predicament, to expose the dangers and pitfalls on man's path and to lead him back to the fold of religion. He does so persuasively because he portrays a world in which the "patience of things" challenges the "impatience of the mind." With the *Hay Wagon* begins a

The Hay Wagon, detail of the central panel.

The Hay Wagon: The Path of Life, *exterior panels of the closed wings.*

The Hawker (The Prodigal Son), about 1510.

phase of metamorphoses and an apotheosis of the sign. A singular audacity, a teeming imagination, and an ambience of magic were needed to reconcile so completely the real with the imaginary, to pit the real against the marvelous, and to transmute the marvelous into the fantastic. Here the subliminal machinery of the whole mannerist conception of the poem-picture was for the first time brought into play.

The central panel and two wings form a trilogy. They illustrate three phases of that elemental theme: the origin, proliferation and punishment of Evil. First, in successive registers on the left wing, we see the fall of the rebel angels, given the forms of insects, scorpions and salamanders streaming down the sky; the creation of Eve; the Temptation and the Fall; the expulsion of the disobedient couple from the earthly paradise. The central panel groups all classes of society around a popular motif of the Low Countries' folklore, the hay wagon (symbol of vanity). It gives pictorial expression to a whole host of popular locutions meaning to "make a fool of" or to cozen: *om tlange hoy plucken* (to grab at the long hay), *met hoey croonen* (to crown with hay), *iemand de kaper vol hooi stoppen* (to stuff someone's cap with hay). All mankind is shown in fond pursuit of its illusions: *Al hoy*, "all hay." But before paying the price of its folly and being exiled to Hell (on the right wing), it has been beset by the Satanic hosts; we see them in the central picture—hideous, hybrid creatures helping to draw the wagon. And when the wings are shut on this world of selfish greed and perversity, there appears the figure of a man who has managed to escape from it. World-weary and bowed down he drags himself along with a basket on his back. This forlorn pilgrim is the first, very summary version of a masterpiece, the famous *Prodigal Son* (Boymans-Van Beuningen Museum, Rotterdam), which would be more correctly entitled *The Hawker*.

This figure too stems from a very ancient tradition and popular locutions. But how masterly is the restraint, the economy of means exemplified in this second version of the theme of the familiar parable! And how well it guards its secret! The more we study it, the more we realize how much eludes us. Here the synthesis of the conceptual and the perceptible is total, absolute, and the whole scene is a delight for the eyes. Its technical expertise is as compelling as the message it conveys. An exquisite handling of an almost monochrome palette implements the subtlest shadings imaginable of beige and grey. They combine to emphasize the indissoluble alliance of figure and landscape: nature reflects the lonely wanderer's nostalgia, which, in turn, is a reflection of the melancholy lot of all mankind.

But who precisely is this wayworn, wraithlike traveler? The Prodigal Son of the parable, prematurely aged by riotous living? Or is it some ordinary vagrant, plodding his weary way? It is both at once, and more as well. The themes are imbricated; we can sense the inner meanings behind the seeming-literal renderings of anecdotal details. This man is in the throes of a cruel dilemma. No, he has not been carousing in the tavern like the Prodigal Son of the parable. He has not herded swine. He has not been squandering his last pennies on harlots: witness the well-lined purse hanging from his belt. Yet, haggard and footsore, he cannot decide what path to choose, torn as he is between the lures of the flesh and the call of "the voice . . . that crieth in the wilderness, Prepare ye the way of the Lord" (Isaiah, XL, 3). Exiled within himself, he wonders what to do, which way to turn. What will be the outcome of this inner conflict? We shall never know. But never, never, can we forget his face.

THE DAWN OF HOPE

A REASSURING FAITH

To love is to escape from doubt and live in
the self-evidence of the heart.

GASTON BACHELARD

Now let us shift our sights and train our eye from an entirely different angle on that "unknown quality of a unique world," of which Proust spoke, and which so well applies to the world of Bosch: a contrapuntal world of many parts and voices, divided aims, all equally insistent yet all maintained in perfect equilibrium. It is this gift of being oneself in many ways that leads to creation of a flawlessly consistent style. Hence the singular aura investing the work of all those great creators who aim at an expression of the world at large, with its virtues and vices, its weaknesses and its grandeur: an aura that, stemming from a private vision, fulfills itself in a personal, selective use of words, sounds, or colors. At this level the poetic quality of the "language," whatever the medium, reigns supreme and identifies the author beyond all doubt, even when by force of circumstances, or of his own volition, his name is absent.

This is why, though unsigned, the Brussels *Crucifixion* reveals the hand of Bosch in every detail. The compact, slender, dematerialized figures, the pale flesh tints, only faintly flushed with pink, the light

The Crucifixion, 1480-1485.

glazes, the dainty brushwork, the muffled tones enlivened with three passages of red—all are distinctive of Bosch's highly personal idiom. All speak the language of his homeland also. The dominant blond tonality gives the landscape—a typically Dutch landscape—an air of languorous repose, imbuing the whole picture with an intimate serenity in keeping with the quietness of the colors, figures and setting. Both its general conception and its execution associate this picture with the

School of Utrecht and, by way of Dirk Bouts, with that of Haarlem. Dating from the end of the 15th century, it keeps to the dimensions of the Primitives. The composition follows a traditional schema. Baldass has aptly observed that the light pink, green and blue used here are typical of the decade 1410-1420. If we are to see this small panel in the right perspective, we must bear in mind that, while contemporary with the last works of Geertgen tot Sint Jans, it also dates to the very time when Gerard David was bringing the Eyckian tradition in Bruges to a close and Quentin Matsys, in Antwerp, renovating the art of the Golden Century in terms of the speculative tendencies and aspirations of the Renaissance. But so effective is the transposition, that it transcends the willful anachronism of the work; natural emotion keeps the lead, and faith safeguards the style. And the crow perched on a dead tree in the background hints at incredulity only to heighten, by contrast, the Christian message of the central theme.

Similarly in the *Marriage at Cana* (Boymans-Van Beuningen Museum, Rotterdam) the artist's inventive genius dominates an archaic style. Quite apart from the highly original layout (the parallel sometimes drawn with Bouts' *Last Supper* in the church of Saint-Pierre at Louvain is unconvincing), the mysterious appeal of this unusual, in some respects ambiguous picture derives from the double meaning imposed on the basic theme and from the symbolism which, in consequence, pervades the rendering of the figures.

The miracle recorded in the Gospel of St John—very freely interpreted—takes place in the center of the composition. A quaint little figure seen from behind, schematic and rectangular, wearing a red wig and an olive green robe, presents the chalice to the bride and bridegroom, and a serene, impassive Christ is blessing it. Physically and morally isolated, the figure of Christ stands out against the patterned gold cloth lining a dais, which he shares with a grave, pensive man, presumably the donor. His august gesture, changing the water into wine, is superbly rendered. It dominates a corrupt gathering of wordlings, votaries of the black arts. For Christ at once arraigns and saves these sinners who are vainly trying to inhabit two incompatible worlds. To bring the indictment home to those who thought they could strike a bargain with Satan, Bosch placed above the Gospel story a quotation from the First Epistle of St Paul to the Corinthians (x, 21): "Ye cannot drink the cup of the Lord, and the cup of devils: ye cannot be partakers of the Lord's table, and of the table of devils."

For the joyous marriage banquet, as we see, is marred by the evil practices of a priest of Satan officiating in the background. Standing beside an altar decked with peculiar objects (a pot, black vases, a mortar, a statuette, *inter alia*) whose esoteric significance has been skillfully elucidated by Fraenger (*Die Hochzeit zu Kana*, Berlin 1950), he points his wand toward the dishes two servants are bringing to the feast. The effect is immediate: the swan on the dish in front spits fire and the boar's head emits a jet of venom. It is clear that Bosch was well acquainted with the ceremonial of the Black Arts. Should we take this to mean he was a member of the notorious sect of the "Free Spirit" and that it was the Grand Master of that secret society who gave him the idea of painting this strange scene? No, the whole psychological atmosphere of the *Marriage* belies any such view. Far from advocating them, the painter plainly aims at stigmatizing the heretical practices in which some members of the *Illustre Vrouwe Broederschap*, the brotherhood in which he held an official post, may have indulged. Quite possibly, too, he got some of the ideas for this scene from the "Swan Banquet" he attended in 1488. In any case, the work is far too complex to yield its meaning at a glance; only close study can unravel its expressive content, its baffling mixture of abstraction and realism, elegance and *bizarrerie*.

The *Adoration of the Magi* (Prado) marks a climactic point in Bosch's œuvre. This triptych well deserves its high renown. It is one of the subtlest picture poems in all Western art. Perhaps the most striking thing about it is the fact that the landscape background occupies no less than four-fifths of the picture space. Flooded with light, it loosens up the clean-cut linearism of the Primitives; decorative calligraphy is

The Marriage at Cana, 1475-1480.

dissolved in gesture and expression, and softened, vibrant colors reproduce the familiar hues of nature. The olive-green of the fields acts as a connecting link between the panels; this chromatic unity is rare in Bosch, the only other instance being the Lisbon *Temptation of St Anthony*. Also, the ochre of the middle distance ensures a homogeneous color register throughout, setting the key of a panoramic development of an entirely novel order, foreshadowing the "cosmic" landscapes of Patinir. The narrative theme occupies the whole width of the central panel. At first sight it appears to present no problems: the Biblical episode seems to be rendered quite straightforwardly. Thirteen days after the Nativity, as related in the Gospel according to St Matthew, there came to Jerusalem three wise men from the east, guided by a star (visible in the blue sky at the top of the central panel). According to the *Golden Legend*, they were kings as well as Magi (i.e. magicians or learned men), hailing from the confines of Persia and Chaldea. Following the star, they entered the house over which it stood, found the young babe with his mother, fell down and worshiped him, and presented their gifts of gold, frankincense and myrrh. Bosch enlarged considerably on the traditional narrative. And in expanding it here he showed much deeper insight than when he composed the earlier *Adoration of the Magi* (in Philadelphia), despite the exceptional freedom of his treatment of the subject in that picture. Though expressed in different terms, the leading idea is the same as that behind the *Marriage at Cana*: faith brings comfort and reassurance, genuine religious feeling will always triumph over the powers of evil. The narrative scenes are packed with topical allusions. Here Bosch keeps to a method he had already tested out successfully: that of creating an organic unity out of multifarious, often conflicting sources.

Moreover, as Charles de Tolnay has pointed out, Bosch has here converted the Adoration of the Magi into a sacrament of the Church, and the entire triptych illustrates the celebration of a Mass, in which the donors on the wings and their patrons (St Joseph on the left, St Agnes on the right) participate. Mary represents the altar; while,

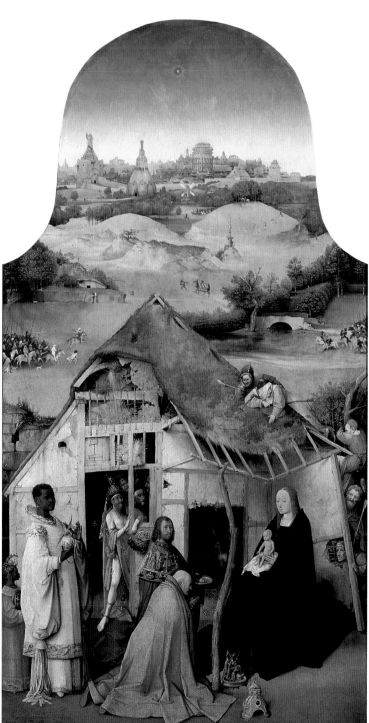

The Adoration of the Magi, triptych, about 1510.

The Adoration of the Magi: Crystal Globe and Bird, *detail of the central panel.*

kneeling in his voluminous red mantle, Balthazar plays the part of the officiating priest, with Melchior and Gaspar acting as his acolytes. Balthazar's gift, the large golden object at the Virgin's feet, at once recalls the Sacrifice of Abraham and prefigures the Crucifixion. It is also crushing down the toads of heresy. The helmet on the ground beside it is adorned with symbols of lust. Melchior is wearing a short metal cape embossed with tiny views of the Queen of Sheba's visit to King Solomon, prototype of the Epiphany. Gaspar, a stately, monumental figure in a magnificent white cloak, is holding in his right hand a white globe faintly tinged with blue, adorned with small figures in grisaille depicting a scene of idolatry.

The group of the three Magi may be regarded as transitional between the temptations of the devil and the Redemption, as Lotte Brand Philip has suggested in a well-documented article in *The Art Bulletin* (December 1953). The decrepit cottage represents at once the stable at Bethlehem, David's hut in ruins, and the sheepfold in the parable of the Good and Bad Shepherds. Just inside in the door is a group of curious figures, oddest of which is the half-naked man, laden with symbols and attributes, with a wound on his leg that can be seen across a transparent bandage. This is the poor leper described in the Babylonian Talmud; also the Jewish Messiah. Quite eager to deliver his people, he is held back by a golden chain, lest he should enter on the scene before the time is ripe. But Bosch has also associated him with the attributes of Antichrist. Inverted, the helmet of Melchior becomes a receptacle of fire; the small bell hanging from a belt decorated with frogs is an emblem of Evil. This helps to explain the singular behavior of the shepherds: they, too, incarnate Evil and instead of worshiping, merely watch and wait. The shining peace of the great open spaces is only briefly ruffled by the little scenes, hinting at the world's unrest, that dapple a tranquil countryside. But—in the words of a great poet, Saint-John Perse—"not always shall we dally in these yellow lands, today's delight."

The Adoration of the Magi: The Fire, *detail of the left panel.*

The Adoration of the Magi: The Bad Shepherds, *detail of the central panel.*

The Crowning with Thorns, 1508-1509.

CRISIS

A TIME OF ANGUISH

A laugh has laughed,
The earth has split,
The sun is up,
A red rift in the sky.
JOHANNES R. BECHER

No, "not always shall we dally in these yellow lands, today's delight." The time of dalliance is over. For Christ is in peril, the devil's hosts are mustering around him. The emissaries of Antichrist have left the golden hut of Bethlehem and lie in ambush on the way to Golgotha.

With Bosch the Stations of the Cross cease to belong to an extra-temporal world and are transposed into the here and now. Bosch felt very strongly about the contamination of Christian doctrine, the sophistries of heresy and their repercussions on the level of contemporary life. From first to last his paintings voice a preacher's message, and a didactic compulsion, active and critical, inspires them. For this man, once regarded as a painter of horror pictures, as a "maker of devils," is a great theologian. His sources are multiple, his store of knowledge is immense. And however he may choose to interpret the material he deals with, always his piety shines through. It is the driving force behind a long, insistent homily whose themes find plenary expression in successive scenes of the Passion.

The Crowning with Thorns (Prado, Madrid), about 1510.

For these scenes are more than a poignant evocation of the sufferings of the Divine Victim; they are a call to order. With extreme concision they voice an agonized protest, a piteous cry of revolt and love. No words are wasted. No trivial anecdotes distract our attention from the leading theme, the inhumanity of Man in the mass. He is shown in close-up, with ruthless precision, and his face reflects his moral degradation. His eyes, nose, mouth, even his garments tell the whole story in crude, outspoken, realistic terms. Yet, within this group of pictures, a dramatic progression, closely allied with the scenic and chromatic techniques successively employed, can be traced. Four (London *Crowning with Thorns*), five (Escorial *Crowning with Thorns*), nine (Princeton *Christ before Pilate*) and then fifteen tormentors (Ghent *Bearing of the Cross*) are seen pressing around the figure of Christ. The human types they body forth gradually change and crystallize; placid and inquisitive at first (London), they develop into boors (Escorial), then grotesques (Princeton), and finally a troop of hideous, ribald fiends (Ghent). And, scene by scene, the expression on Christ's face changes from sadness to bitterness, from bitterness to anguish, from anguish to suffering unspeakable.

Christ before Pilate, 1513-1515.

Ecce Homo, 1480-1485.

The series of Passion paintings, unique in the world of art, seems to have a prelude, a theatrical prelude—almost one might say a "curtain-raiser"—in the *Ecce Homo* at the Staedel Institute in Frankfort (there is a variant in the Boston Museum of Fine Arts). Linked up with it is the *Ecce Homo* in the Philadelphia Museum of Art. Both have a setting reminiscent of the stage. They seem to us to illustrate a period of the painter's career whose climax may well be marked by the *Marriage at Cana*. Roggen has rightly observed that the Philadelphia

The Mocking of Christ, about 1480.

Ecce Homo (fragment of a composition originally much higher than it now is) seems to have been inspired by the float representing "Christ Scourged" in the annual procession held at Bois-le-Duc. As for the Frankfort *Ecce Homo*, its arrangement seems to us to derive from a popular stage performance of scenes of the Passion. Plainer than ever here are the indications of an actual stage set which Marcel Brion has detected in the *Seven Deadly Sins*. The praetorium before which Christ stands gives the impression of a flimsy pasteboard structure imitating brickwork, erected for the occasion on a public thoroughfare. Its artificial character is stressed by the convincingly realistic vista and quiet, spacious avenue of the townscape forming the background. But this theatrical element in the presentation of the scene does not rule out the possibility that Bosch may also have drawn on the repertory of popular imagery and derived inspiration from some print or picture dealing with the same theme. Rejecting the sources proposed by Dvorak (Schongauer's "Passion") and by de Tolnay (a lost work by the Master of Flémalle), Jacques Combe has drawn attention to a woodcut, executed in a provincial style, which he has recently discovered and which has unmistakable analogies with Bosch's painting.

Here, the scenic disposition of the picture elements justifies the arbitrary relation between figures and background, the drastic separation of the composition into two halves, and the dislocation of the two figure groups, one on the "stage," one in the "pit." On the one hand we have the complacent arrogance of the Pharisees thrusting Christ forward and exhibiting him to the mob; and, on the other, the furious hatred of that mob, expressed by all the cruel, bestial faces gazing up at him. Also the garments help to point the contrast between the facial expressions of the two groups: the semi-oriental garb of Christ's persecutors; the rich Brabantine costumes in the fashion of the day, worn by the leaders of the mob below. This dualism conforms to the dialectic already employed to such striking effect by Van Ouwater and Geertgen tot Sint Jans. Here, however, the emotive implications of the scene are kept under by its essentially "theatrical" presentation. The secondary characters mime but do not really live their parts. And this lack of real emotion is paralleled by a deficiency of plastic qualities: sketchy modeling, turgid drawing, awkward gestures, dim profiles, clumsily rendered hands. These shortcomings indicate that the picture was an early work. This is confirmed by the need the artist felt to add inscriptions, as though the picture could not speak for itself. *Ecce Homo*, says Pilate, and his words are written on the upper left of the panel, while the mob's answering cry, *Crucifige eum*, is inscribed above their heads: *Salva nos Christus redemptor* is the prayer of the two donors originally shown kneeling in the left foreground, but now painted out. The symbolism, too, is imperfectly integrated and sets the tone of the work only in a very superficial way. Indeed the toad on the large buckler on the right, the owl perched in the tiny window of the praetorium, the crescent on the flag hanging from the town hall in the background, tend to submerge, rather than to emphasize, the general effect at which the painter aimed. The work was meant to edify. It still does—it did so in its day—but it does nothing more.

Perhaps as many as twenty-five or thirty years elapsed between the Frankfort *Ecce Homo* and the Ghent *Bearing of the Cross*. A comparison of the two works enables us the better to appreciate the extraordinary degree of refinement, plenitude and intensity achieved by Bosch toward the close of his career. A personal sense of imminent catastrophe, heightened no doubt by contemporary rumors of the impending "end of the world," quickened the visionary inspiration impregnating the latter work. Bosch was keenly conscious—none more than he—of the mood of brooding apprehension that prevailed in the towns and countryside of Northern Europe as the year 1500 drew near. That a similar disquiet was felt in the great humanist centers of Italy has been ably demonstrated by André Chastel (*Art et Humanisme à Florence au temps de Laurent le Magnifique*, Paris 1959). But the "feeling that an age was drawing to its close" does not seem to have been counterbalanced in the North by any "expectation of a glorious renewal." As the 15th century ended and the 16th began, the dawn of the Renaissance had not yet shed any ray of light upon the temperamental gloom of the northern Low Countries.

Only if we know something of the moral and intellectual climate then prevailing in the Netherlands can we understand the bitter indignation, pessimism and high-strung emotionalism that find expression in the elliptical, lapidary style of the Ghent *Bearing of the Cross*, a work which springs—to use the words of Mikel Dufrenne in a different context—from "a life of single-minded dedication, from the indefinable correlation that exists between the actions of an individual and, by the same token, between the situations in which he finds himself involved and the faces the world confronts him with." But the *Bearing of the Cross* is located in a world beyond the world, a space that is not space, a seventh Hell. The whole work is a tissue of unprecedented abbreviations. All that does not bear directly on its tragic theme is deliberately omitted. Against a backdrop of a darkness so dense as to seem almost palpable, looms a nightmarish assemblage of bestial, bloated, grimacing faces, twisted out of human semblance by cruelty and hatred.

It is clear that the artist gave much thought to rendering the characteristic expressions of these faces. Some authorities have suggested that they may derive from the masks worn in processions, mystery plays and carnivals. Support is lent to this theory by the fact that Bosch is often mentioned in the archives of Bois-le-Duc as taking part in plays and pageants organized by the Brotherhood of Our Lady. Yet it is hard to believe that Bosch resorted to any such expedient. The mask is too obviously a mechanical contrivance and its set grimace can never convey the human quality of a real face treated expressively, greatly distorted perhaps, but essentially *alive*. And if the faces of the crowd escorting Christ are as horrifying as hellfire itself, the reason is that Bosch has evoked them from the depths of the human personality and they embody feelings always lurking in its demon-haunted under-world.

The Bearing of the Cross, 1515-1516.

The Bearing of the Cross: Veronica, *detail.*

The Bearing of the Cross: The Penitent Thief and the Dominican, *detail*.

Not a single gaze is directed toward the center of the scene. No one pays any heed to the Divine Victim, whose eyes are closed in mournful contemplation of some inner vision. Deathly pale and haggard, the Penitent Thief seems to be groaning with disgust at the rantings of a ghoulish Dominican. At the opposite corner of the picture, in contrapposto, we see the pale, ethereal figure of Veronica, personification of the Church, who is holding out before her the miraculous veil.

That this picture has been carefully thought out in every detail is evident in the unusual arrangement of the figures, their unlooked-for attitudes, the telling contrasts of sobriety and violence, resignation and truculence, calm and passion. But we feel, too, that the painter brought to his work an intense personal emotion, sublimated by his genius onto a universal plane. No less admirable is the subtle handling of the colors and it is on them, in large measure, that the style hinges. Ranging from madder-red, claret, vermilion, saffron yellows, to sparkling blues, steel gray, livid greens, gleaming whites and iridescent ochres, there is a constant play of prismatic effects, alternations of warm and cool tones, a kaleidoscopic variety of chromatic modulations. Only a total mastery of the medium could ensure such exquisite results, could thus dematerialize the surface texture and render color so amazingly limpid, so lavishly suffused with light. Even Van Mander was struck by this fluidity. "Bosch," he wrote, "greatly stressed the underpainting with an eye to the general effect." This remark might seem to apply equally well to many Flemish or Netherlandish masters. Yet it is peculiarly appropriate to Bosch. And the technical examination carried out when the painting was under laboratory treatment in 1957 confirmed Van Mander's remark. It revealed the fact that the ground had been prepared with exceptional care. This ground preparation consisted of a double coat of chalk and animal glue, the thinnest, most tenuous so far observed in the work of any northern Primitive. Contrary to classical practice, Bosch applied but a single coat of paint, again extremely thin, over a schematic underdrawing. Such is the secret of one of the most remarkable effects of transparency ever achieved by any painter.

Ecce Homo and The Bearing of the Cross. Drawing.

Sheet of sketches with Monsters.

THE CENTER OF GRAVITY

FANTASY RUNS RIOT

To comprehend the singing of the toads
The teeming life of insects
The pure and regulated heat of summer
The harsh winds of old winter
A dead and living world.

PAUL ÉLUARD

SUPERSTITION is the anteroom of fear. But an obsession with sin, no less than the "sleep of reason," engenders monsters. Hence this nightmare world bearing the name of Bosch, the demon called desire, a wild debauch of fantasy run riot. Everything breaks up, falls asunder, scatters, then is reassembled. Lagoons of honey, skies like topsy-turvy seas, pools of darkness. A mad world of smoking bagpipes, broken globes and tangled tentacles. Fish swim in the air and angels roam the earth. Strawberries and raspberries large as melons tempt the eye. Fires, flames, dust and ashes, gleams of lurid light. Spikes, spines and arrows, swords, knives and daggers, prick, pierce and flay. Malignant flowers, fiery thorns and "slimy things with legs." Broken eggs, flying foetuses, armor-plated scorpions. Men with snouts for noses, bellies crawling snailwise; phosphorescent gourds creeping on cats' feet. Glassy eyes, jaws of Hell. Lewd banquets, hideous embraces, eerie miscegenations. All is foundering in a cosmic shipwreck. The powers of evil are on the warpath and no quarter given. By what strange magic has Bosch contrived to make the horrible enchanting, the shapeless shapely, the graceless graceful, ugliness sublime? What is he aiming at in these extravagances? What is the source of this incessant spate of plastic invectives? Are Bosch's pictures the "fevers dappled with the tulip-trees of a dream," of which the poet Saint-John Perse speaks? Or do these "clouds of insects, fluttering up into the blue—like tattered scraps of holy texts," represent *disjecta membra* of holy texts? Yes, such they are beyond all doubt. Tags of sermons, scraps of Bible lore, images from the Lives of the Saints, gleanings from the Apocalypse, passages from the Golden Legend, excerpts from the *Visio Tondali*, from the writings of St Augustine (*De divinatione daemonum*) and St Bernard (*Apologia ad Guillelmum*), from Jan van Ruysbroeck (*The Four Temptations, The Spiritual Tabernacle*), from Albertus Magnus (*De Animalibus, Summa theologica, Scriptum super libros Sententiarum*)—these were no doubt the literary sources of Bosch's fantastic art. Nor can we understand it fully without consulting the homilies of Dionysius van Rijckel (*Liber de quatuor hominum novissimis*) and Jean Gerson (*De diversis diaboli tentationibus*), the revelations of Alain de La Roche (*Alanus redivivus*), whose disciple was Jakob Sprenger, the Dominican inquisitor at Cologne and one of the authors of the famous *Malleus maleficarum*, a manual on sorcery for the use of inquisitors, containing a full description, in the most lurid terms, of the witches and wizards whom "God, angered by the world's corruption, has permitted the devil to let loose on earth."

As early as the 12th century, a dark strain of unkempt fancies had worked its way insidiously into the contemplative life. St Bernard saw the danger and issued a solemn warning. "What are those ridiculous monstrosities doing in the cloisters where the monks read and study? To what purpose are those unclean apes, those fierce lions, those monstrous centaurs, those half-men? You see one head attached to several bodies, or one body to several heads. Here is a quadruped with a dragon's tail, there a dragon with a quadruped's tail. Here is a horse ending as a goat, there a horned animal ending as a horse. Wherever one turns there is such a strange profusion of forms; men study these marble simulacra rather than their books and spend their days poring on such things as these instead of meditating on the laws of God. O God, if we are not ashamed of these absurdities, let us at least be ashamed of the thoughts that they call up!" The warning fell on deaf ears. As the Middle Ages drew to a close, men came more and more under the thrall of these suggestive images, of diabolic fantasies which, while professing to depict the agonies of the damned, pandered to their carnal appetites.

Alain de La Roche, a Dominican visionary from Brittany, was living in the Netherlands and Bosch may well have heard him preach (he died at Zwolle in 1475). He typifies the warped and freakish piety of the 15th century, the *devotio moderna* and the "ultra-concrete" expression it gave to religious sentiment. His writings, consisting for the most part of sermons and highly colored descriptions of his visions, are remarkable for their plethora of sexual imagery. In his mind's eye he saw "beasts personifying the sins of the flesh, equipped with fearsome genital organs and belching streams of fire whose billowing smoke darkened the earth; he saw the *meretrix apostasiae*, the whore of apostasy, spawning apostates, devouring them, vomiting them up again, then embracing, fondling them like a mother" (Huizinga, *The Waning of the Middle Ages*).

Then there was the great Flemish theologian Dionysius van Rijckel, founder of the Carthusian monastery at Bois-le-Duc. He too, while denouncing the obscenity and license that had crept into religious festivals, sought to excite the fear of God's wrath by detailed and vivid accounts of the punishments in store for sinners. His evocations of Hell were nothing if not lurid. It was an "infernal Gehenna, third of the Four Last Things, a salutary remembrance of which preserves from sin." "Try to imagine," he continued, "a white-hot oven and in the oven a naked man doomed to stay there for all eternity. Would not the mere sight of such torment seem to us unbearable? How pitiable would we deem the lot of such a man! Picture to yourselves how he would struggle to escape from the oven, how he would groan and scream with pain! Think what his life would be like and what excruciating mental anguish he would also suffer once he realized this dreadful punishment would never, never end!" (Huizinga, *op. cit.*)

These brief passages are typical. They have not been chosen for their pungency, and they stand out little if at all from their context. And they suffice to show how the crusade against Evil had fired the moralists' imagination. No doubt they felt that, if their words were to take effect on the sensibility of the populace, shock tactics were called for. True, these hysterical injunctions were perhaps overcharged with the fantastic element. But in any case, there was little hope of weaning the populace from their belief in witchcraft, in the most extravagant pretensions of black magic, in the occult powers of alchemists. The papal bull *Summis desiderantes affectibus*, issued in 1494 *contra sectam maleficiorum*, while denouncing these malpractices in outspoken terms, recognized that commerce with the Evil One was feasible. "Many persons of both sexes," we read in one notable passage, "heedless of their own salvation and departing from the Catholic faith, have intercourse with demons, incubi and succubi; and by spells, incantations and other unspeakable excesses of superstition and sorcery, and by heinous crimes, they succeed in sterilizing and destroying the foetuses of women and animals, the fruits of the earth and trees... Moreover, they visit and torment men, women and animals with all sorts of aches and pains, internal and external... They beguile Christians into denying with their own mouths their faith in holy baptism, and their victims fear not to perpetrate unspeakable crimes and excesses, goaded on thereto by the enemy of the human kind; this they do at the peril of their souls, with great offense to the divine majesty, and moreover set the multitude a scandalous example" (quoted in E. Castelli, *Le Démoniaque dans l'art*, Paris 1959).

A more detailed analysis of the climate of the age might perhaps bring out more clearly the influence of his environment on the painter's attitude to life. But it would not suffice to reveal the wellsprings of his art. The moral background and the literary sources fail to throw any real light on the passage from idea to pictured image. Nor do they in any way explain the thoroughgoing originality of Bosch's fantastic demonology. They are at most the groundwork of a dream: a dream oriented by a will to power together with a will to action; a dream that only engendered monsters so as the better to bring home to the populace the sin of "crooked thinking." Despite its seeming incoherence this dream reflects the basic integrity of a thoroughly logical mind whose constant purpose was to restore its spiritual unity, its psychic equilibrium and its physical cohesion to the social order. This is one of the reasons why even the strangest collocations of images in Bosch's art fall into a steady rhythm and follow a uniform directive. These composite pictures are unlike any others. Whether satanic or paradisiac, the images contained in them have no analogies of form, spirit or color with the Romanesque teratology. Gothic bestiaries, Burgundian illuminations, the flying monsters of the Campo Santo in Pisa, or the tangled bodies of the Damned in Rogier van der Weyden's vision of Hell (Hôtel-Dieu, Beaune). Bosch may have found some helpful suggestions in the prevailing art tradition, but he directly borrowed nothing from it. Except in a few particular instances, to which we shall refer at a later page, he invented everything; and his inventions sprang from an inner compulsion closely bound up with the life force of the *Zeitgeist*. (We are unable to agree with certain writers on the subject who have overhastily assumed that the gargoyles of the cathedral of Bois-le-Duc and the great fires that on several occasions swept the city were the major sources of his inspiration. The arguments in favor of this theory hardly meet the case; indeed any such mechanistic explication of Bosch's art must surely be rejected. Even if we accept Fraenger's view that in his large-scale works Bosch conformed to detailed "programs" imposed on him by the sect of which he was a member, the fact remains that he brought a truly prodigious and free-ranging imagination to bear on them.)

In short, none of these theories provides satisfactory answers to the fundamental problems set by the "case" of Bosch. When all is said and done, on what is this vast profusion of imagery based? His eerie figures live and breathe, but whence comes their amazing vitality? There is no denying that the world Bosch shows us is a world of dreams. Can these strange visions have been due to drug-taking? Dare we assume that the painter resorted to some phantasmogenic drug so as to give free rein to his subconscious self and attain one of those "abysses of the psyche" to which Henri Michaux had access under the influence of mescaline? As it so happens, a recent discovery lends support to this theory. Professor Peuckert of Göttingen University unearthed the recipe for a stimulant named "witches' pomatum" in a 16th-century book, made some, and tested it on several persons. All, after a deep sleep of twenty hours, had the same tale to tell; all had dreamed of flying, of orgies in the company of satanic creatures, of visits to the netherworld. To suggest that Bosch may have used similar means to attain a region of the personality normally inaccessible, is in no way to belittle the value of his work. Far from impairing the creative faculties, drugs can stimulate them. Rimbaud, Huxley, Artaud and Michaux in our own time testify to this. But, even so, how can we fail to be impressed by the patient labor and exacting craftsmanship needed to give concrete visual form to these strange adventures in the hinterlands of consciousness and to enable others to participate in them? Nor must we overlook the fact that the images drawn from a purely imaginary world are usually associated with images deriving from a given theme or a written text, converted into plastic terms, then charged with new meanings. Thus a conscious symbolism is grafted onto archetypes which, as Jung has shown, belong to the collective unconscious of mankind. Generally speaking, each sign carries several meanings, which a mysterious energy has crytallized into an organic whole. This presupposes a latent, activating faculty of reason which reason cannot explain, but depth psychology could perhaps account for. Assuredly it is not due to chance that, from the *Hay Wagon* to the *Garden of Earthly Delights* (Prado), from the *Last Judgment* (Academy of Fine Arts, Vienna) to the *Temptation of St Anthony* (National Museum, Lisbon), the theme of fire so constantly recurs: fire smoldering under the embers, setting a countryside aflame, lighting up space. When man desires a radical change, as Gaston Bachelard has pointed out, he resorts to fire. "Fire implies the will to make a 'clean sweep,' to speed up time, to hasten all life toward its end, to an afterlife" (*La Psychanalyse du feu*, Paris 1938). Moreover, from the psychoanalytic viewpoint, fire is a symbol of sin and evil. Seen from this angle, Bosch's demonology proves to be more purposive, didactic, more critical of contemporary abuses, and his choice of subjects more precisely motivated than was once supposed. By the same token, the underlying logic of his œuvre gains in force, nobility and scope, and we can discern more clearly the substructure on which his thought is founded.

But there is more. "Fire," we are told, "is the great connecting link between all symbols. It joins mind and matter, vice and virtue. It idealizes materialist knowledge; materializes idealistic knowledge. It is the *modus operandi* of an essential ambiguity" (G. Bachelard, *op. cit.*). It keys up the impulses of opposition and contradiction, and leads the dreaming mind to combine the most conflicting elements in a single image. Thus, in some peculiar manner it seems to convey the double meanings characteristic of the earliest phase of language—when the same word had two meanings, one the exact contrary of the other. (This phenomenon of double meaning, philologists tell us, can be traced back to the oldest word-roots.) Thus Bosch's approach to painting would seem to derive from a profound understanding of the workings of the primitive mind, and the latent ambivalence of his work to reflect the original, basic ambiguity of man's imagination and, by extension, of the human condition in general.

This hypothesis may explain, to some extent, the hold which the theme of the Temptation of St Anthony certainly had on Bosch's mind. Anthony, patron saint of the Order of Antonites, was one of the most popular saints of the later Middle Ages—a period when popularity of this order involved not only a cult of the saint in question, but led also to a proliferation of far-fetched legends and perverse interpretations

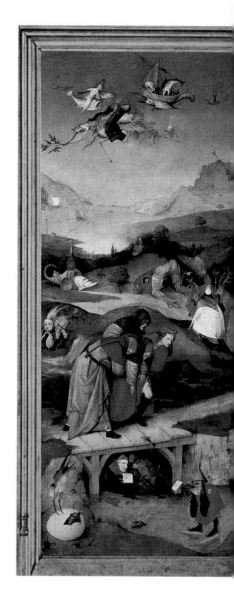

The Temptation of St Anthony:
The Arrest of Christ *and* The Bearing of the Cross,
exterior panels of the closed wings.

of his functions. St Anthony was an early victim of this phenomenon. Long invoked as a guardian against certain diseases, he now came to be regarded as author of the very maladies he was called on to cure! (Thus erysipelas was popularly known as "St Anthony's fire.") Henceforth he was more feared than worshiped. The spokesmen of divine justice seldom retain their integrity in popular conceptions of their ministry.

The Temptation of St Anthony, triptych, about 1505.

This goes far to explain the extent to which pagan superstitions were carried over into Christian ethics.

In many imprecations the saint figures as a demonic fire-raiser: "May St Anthony burn me!"; "St Anthony burn the brothel"; "St Anthony burn the steed!" Such locutions evidence both the fear in which he was held, and a smoldering resentment against him. They

The Temptation of St Anthony:
The Wheel, *detail of the central panel.*

also illustrate that obsession with fire which is so marked a psychic factor in Bosch's art and which culminated in the superb *Temptation of St Anthony* in the National Museum of Ancient Art in Lisbon.

Keeping to the layout for which he always had a predilection, Bosch spread the theme over three panels, and here the compositional and coloristic unity of the parts is as flawless as in the Prado *Adoration of the Magi.* The guiding ideas can be traced to the life of St Anthony

The Temptation of St Anthony:
The Alchemical Child, *detail of the central panel.*

as told by Athanasius and recapitulated in the Golden Legend. Scion
of a wealthy family, he divided the estate he had inherited with his
sister, sold his own share and distributed the money to the poor. He
then withdrew to a cavern in the desert to medidate on the teachings
of Christ. One day "a sudden din burst on his ears, the walls shook,
and a horde of fiends swarmed around him in animal shapes, roaring,
howling, hissing, snarling. Lions, tigers, wolves, snakes, scorpions,

bears and dragons sought to overwhelm the faith of the poor hermit, assailed on all sides by obscene gesturings and evil thoughts. Then, finding these of no avail, they changed their tactics. They wooed him with the softest blandishments, in the guise of beautiful women. Sometimes, too, they resorted to intimidation; launching at him huge and hideous giants or ruthless bands of soldiers..."

The Lisbon triptych shows obvious traces of this colorful account of Anthony's tribulations—an account that must have seemed to an

The Temptation of St Anthony:

◁ The Heretics, *detail of the left panel.*

▷ The Hollow Tree, *detail of the right panel.*

imaginative painter an ideal pretext for an exercise in demonology *à outrance*. Bosch's interpretation went far beyond the letter of the original, and also departed from the established iconography. Closely bound up with the ideological climate of the times (the spread of superstition, belief in the devil, predictions of catastrophes and pestilence, an obsession with witchcraft and the Seven Deadly Sins, a partial return to the Hebrew concept of Satan as the instrument of God, etc.), Bosch's version of the theme brought into play a whole system of symbols charged with allusions to black magic and alchemy, both of which, it is important to remember, were saturated through and through with sexual imagery inspired by fire. So many forms and ideas stemming from conflicting frames of reference intersect that some details are almost incomprehensible, and experts have been exploring this mausoleum of dead hieroglyphs for several decades. The research work begun by de Tolnay, Jacques Combe and Bax has been much advanced by Castelli (1952), Charles D. Cuttler (1957) and Wilhelm Fraenger (1957).

Still, whatever approach be taken, we come to much the same conclusion. Behind the frenzied diabolism, behind the riot of phantasmagoric forms, we sense a profound, deeply poignant pessimism. Traversed by opposing lines of force, the world Bosch figures forth becomes a pandemonium, under the thrall of Satan. The laws of nature have collapsed, the devil has obliterated the distinctions between Truth and Lies. Midway between the hell fires ravaging the earth and the waters engulfing it, St Anthony has thought to find peace and solitude "in an abandoned fort beyond the Nile, now crawling with serpents." No sooner is he there than he is beset by a witches' sabbath. But he is deaf to the tumult, unmoved by malefic spells and fleshly temptation, blind to fiendish parodies of the Mass. Unperturbed, he prays, blesses and stands firm. His faith is unshakeable. He is morally isolated, halfway between Christ, visible on a crucifix at the back of his hermitage, and the magician in a red cloak and top hat, master of the unholy revels, nonchalantly leaning on a parapet a few paces behind him. A black mass is being said. Standing behind a round table, a high priestess whose mitre is a seething mass of thorns and vipers offers the eucharistic chalice to a musician with a pig's snout and an owl perched on his head. Like the owl, says Ruysbroeck, are "all those who resist pure truth and wholesome doctrine, seeking out new opinions and inventions wherewith to obfuscate the law of God" (*Spiritual Tabernacle*, Ch. 132). Fraenger thinks that the wine in the proffered cup is snake poison and relates to a passage in the Old Testament: "For their vine is of the vine of Sodom, and of the fields of Gomorrah; their grapes are grapes of gall, their clusters are bitter: Their wine is the poison of dragons, and the cruel venom of asps" (Deuteronomy, XXXII, 32-33).

The Temptation of St Anthony: The Round Table, *detail of the central panel.*

Seated in front of St Anthony is a curious, trunkless man, his legs attached directly to a large head wrapped in a dark turban. This "head-and-legs" figure recurs frequently in Bosch's work. Here we have a *gryllus*, a fantastic being often found in imagery of the day. It is believed to derive from an ancient prototype, whose originator, according to Pliny, was Antiphilos the Egyptian, a contemporary of Apelles. The revival of this motif in the closing years of the 15th century met with such widespread favor that "it may well be wondered," writes Baltrušaitis, "whether it was not directly related to the Renaissance. Very precocious in the schools of the North, anyhow as regards certain

The Temptation of St Anthony: The Ruins, *detail of the central panel.*

themes, the Renaissance began by a predilection for the monstrous and fantastic and issued directly from the Middle Ages" (see *Le Moyen Age fantastique*, Paris 1955). Baltrušaitis' observation is all the more pertinent in view of the fact that the motif in question was alluded to (under the name of *grillo*) in a Spanish work, first published in 1560, in which Bosch is mentioned for the first time (Don Felipe de Guevara, *Comentarios de la Pintura*, published by Ponz, Madrid 1788).

Standing in fetid, greenish water, a tonsured demon is reciting the black mass. Two pseudo-monks stand beside him, one with an inverted funnel on his head (symbol of madness), the other with a bird's nest

The Temptation of St Anthony: The Black Mass, detail of the central panel.

on top of which is an egg (symbol of alchemy). The egg, Jacques Combe reminds us, not only alludes to the oval crucible in which the philosopher's stone is concocted, but also stands for the world-egg out of which, according to the alchemists, the universe was hatched. The egg appears again and again: on the platter held up by a black servant; scuttling along on bird's legs across the shattered vault above the hermit's cell; winging its way through the sky. And the huge green and red gourd, making so fine a color patch in the left foreground, is an allusion to the boiler of the alchemist's still, sometimes called in old texts "the philosopher's cucurbit" (i.e. flask or gourd). Devils are pouring out of it. One of them, wearing a flowing green cloak, is sitting astride a big turtle and "profaning the angelic harp." Two groups of figures, balancing each other, are arrayed on either side of the central motif. Each includes a sinister personage whose head is encased in a dry, hollow, pointed tree-trunk (another symbol of the alchemist's furnace). This symbolism is made abundantly clear by the image of the tree-woman bestriding a huge rat (symbol of falsehood, according to Ruysbroeck, *Spiritual Tabernacle*). She carries in her arms (which end in dead branches) the "philosophical child," fruit of the union effected by the philosopher's stone. Flying through the air above is a boat with the neck and head of a swan: it symbolizes the "young man who, with no fear of God, indulges his natural appetites and leads a life of sensual pleasure" (Ruysbroeck, *op. cit.*).

But human endurance has its limits. On the left wing we see the limp figure of the saint, who has lost consciousness, being carried away by two monks and a peasant. Forming a graceful arabesque, the group stands out against some rolling hills, unviolated by the witches' sabbath; the outline of this fragment of undesecrated nature exactly corresponds to that of the group of the four men, whose profound dejection is conveyed by their attitudes alone. This beautifully conceived fragment has the poignancy of a Station of the Cross. It is an interesting point that the peasant with the blue head-cloth (a portrait of the painter?) has exactly the same face as the hapless wanderer on

The Temptation of St Anthony:
The Alchemist's Still, *detail of the central panel.*

the outer panels of the *Hay Wagon* triptych and the *Hawker* in the Boymans-Van Beuningen Museum, Rotterdam. There are other prefigurations here of the latter painting. In the middle of the left wing an obscenely crouching man has transformed St Anthony's hut into a bordello; the grass growing on his back and the branches sprouting

The Temptation of St Anthony, details of the left panel: △ St Anthony Fainting Away.
▷ The Devil's Messenger.

from his legs indicate, as Charles D. Cuttler has pointed out, that he is "rooted in sin." The tiny figure of a woman at the window, the barrel and the staff propped against the eaves, all reappear in front of the tavern, obviously a house of ill fame, in the Rotterdam *Hawker*.

Fish with men on their backs are sailing in the sky: grotesque counterparts of the flying carpet of the Arabian Nights—man's age-old dream of the conquest of the air. His hands clasped in prayer, the saint is lying flat on the back of a winged toad. A ship mounted on a flying

The Temptation of St Anthony:
Sailing Monsters, *detail of the left panel.*

whale and manned by a fiendish crew escorts him. Another flying fish appears in the righthand panel, piloted by a fat man with an egg-shaped body. He stands for the sin of gluttony, also exemplified below, in the foreground, by a table spread with wine and food. The saint is as impervious to its lure as to that of a naked girl in front of him, standing knee-deep in water within a hollow tree. The insistence, everywhere apparent, on such elemental themes, dominants of medieval thought,

The Temptation of St Anthony:
The Town, *detail of the right panel.*

as earth and water, fire and air, heat and cold, moisture and dryness, indicate the cosmic nature of Bosch's conception. Yet, behind the proliferation of dream-begotten forms and fancies, we can sense that cool, critical spirit which was soon to give rise to a wholly new outlook on life. The Lisbon triptych is at once an ultimate attempt to revitalize a decaying humanism and an intriguing prelude to the Renaissance. In 1509 Erasmus published his *Moriae encomium* (Praise of Folly), in which

The Garden of Earthly Delights, about 1505.
Eden, *left panel, and* Musical Hell, *right panel.*

he satirized "those silly people who never tire of listening to preposterous tales of specters, ghosts, evil spirits and hell fire."

Once again Bosch gave free scope to his teeming imagination in that extraordinary work commonly called the *Garden of Earthly Delights* (Prado), his largest triptych.

Nowhere else, in the whole field of art, do we find such a teeming profusion and diversity of images and signs, or a comparable alliance of the marvelous (left wing and central panel) with the fantastic (right

The Garden of Earthly Delights, central panel.

The Garden of Earthly Delights: Eden, *two details of the left panel.*

wing). Everything in this famous triptych is at once a delight to the eye and a puzzle to the mind. So much is conveyed *sub rosa* that, despite the ingenious interpretations, backed by erudite arguments, that we owe to some recent exegetes, we can scarcely hope to pluck out the heart of its mystery. If we are not to lose our bearings in this maze of imagery, we do best, perhaps, to begin by studying the picture with our *eyes*, without seeking to penetrate its secrets. No one who does so can escape the spell cast by the style of the central panel—perhaps the most singular, most fascinating expression of the genius of this great artist that has come down to us.

"In Praise of Lust," that central panel might well be called. For the exposition of his theme, the painter has adopted the vertical layout of medieval tapestries. Three well-defined zones, one above the other, suggest spatial recession: soft green below, greenish yellow in the middle distance, then a tract of blue sky and water framed in light ochre. These basic tonalities provide the setting for a delightful counterpoint of colors, whose clearest notes are bright, translucent reds and blues. This is the most gayly colored picture Bosch ever painted. The pigment is mat, thinner, lighter, more tenuous than ever, and —now that the panel has been cleaned of varnish—gives an illusion of tempera painting. No less harmonious are the color nuances of the left wing, and the scene depicted, while quieter and simpler, breathes the same fervor, the same tenderness. But the right wing strikes a very different note. Its color-scheme is somber, composed of cold tones of blue-black, leaden-gray and purplish blue, interspersed with pools of darkness and silence, lurid gleams of red and yellow.

The Garden of Earthly Delights: The Fountain of Youth, *detail of the central panel.*

In the central panel graceful forms and lovely colors realize the poet's dream of an "artificial paradise" glittering with all the flowers of evil. Amorous encounters, lovers' picnics, banquets of strawberries and cherries—all the senses are glutted in a languorous expanse of green lawns and shady thickets. Voluptuous embraces, eager glances, innocent or lascivious frolics, swimming parties, merry dances. Plants, flowers and birds share in the love-making; it is as if all nature were bathed in a heady, aphrodisiac fragrance. And yet—somehow there is nothing repulsive or unwholesome in the scene. Bosch never lapses into what passes for "bad taste" or vulgarity. Even his most scabrous inventions have a curious dignity, an elegance of their own, a simple, natural appeal. For the purely physical aspects of these naked figures are clad with a poetic glamour. His far-ranging imagination endows this magician of the brush with a unique power of converting crude realities into the stuff of dreams. The frail, elongated bodies have neither weight nor fleshly substance. Treated in the Gothic manner, with slim waists and narrow shoulders, these men and women seem disembodied, dematerialized. Linearism prevails over modeling, the arabesque over realism, abstract eroticism over sensuality, daintiness of gesture over suggestive attitudes, mind over physical pleasure, the fairy tale over the factual. Thus the innocent realities of the tale Bosch tells us are transmuted into the fabulous. This effect is largely due to a procedure which consists in a reversal of the order of nature; human figures are relatively small, while plants and animals bulk larger than life. Yet the coherence of the real world is not impaired by these gigantic birds, huge mussels, flowers and fruit, and monstrous fish. Though proportions are changed by these enlargments, there is no metathesis of forms, no break of continuity in the structure of the dreamworld Bosch evokes. All is so adroitly planned that the paradoxical becomes the plausible.

A curious piquancy is added to the style by the contrast between the delicate fragility of the figures and their setting of clawlike plants, jagged rocks, thorny flowers and foliage, made, one would say, to

The Garden of Earthly Delights: The Alchemical Marriage, *detail of the central panel.*

The Garden of Earthly Delights: The Creation of the World,
exterior panels of the closed wings.

scratch and tear the naked flesh of the lighthearted denizens of this enchanted garden.

The flamboyant decorative calligraphy of landscape and figures is diversified by a series of opaque or transparent mobile spheres: glass balls and globes, little worlds apart, just big enough to hold a pair of lovers. This is, indeed, the picture's central theme and it may well have an ontological significance, basic to a new conception of the cosmos (see G. Bachelard, *La Poétique de l'espace*, Paris 1957). We have already noted the frequency of this motif in Bosch's pictures, and as Baltrušaitis suggests, the theme of human figures shut up in glass jars may well relate not only to "the degeneration of the crystalline cosmos, but also to an oriental fable concerning hell. It will be remembered that Buddha imprisoned the youngest son of Kwei-tsu Mu, mother of ten thousand demons, in a glass alms vase shaped like a globe. A belief that devils could be shut up in phials was prevalent in the Middle Ages, but the earliest known illustration of the theme figures on a Chinese handscroll of the 11th century where there is a horde of demons prefiguring the Gothic Tartarus" (*op. cit.*).

This brings us to another problem, that of the intriguing composition representing the *Creation*, seen on the outside of the triptych when the wings are closed. It takes the form of a huge, semi-transparent globe bisected on the plane of the equator and containing a magnificent landscape painted in grisaille (or, as Fraenger suggests, a picture of the state of the world immediately before the Millennium). De Tolnay, who was the first to publish it (1937), commented on the fact that in this remarkable depiction of the primeval world we have the first "pure" landscape in art—or, more precisely, in *European* art. For the right-hand portion in particular is treated in a manner so delicate, so vaporous and suggestive that it cannot fail to remind us of Far-Eastern inkwash painting, the poetic landscapes of the Sung period. Some years ago attention was also drawn to the analogies with Chinese painting in certain details of the background of the Prado *Adoration of the Magi* (see *Miscellanea Leo van Puyvelde*, Brussels 1949). To our mind, however, these resemblances are very slight. Photographic reproduction in black and white may give an illusory impression of similarities with Chinese art, but this is dispelled when we study the picture itself. But in the *Creation* the resemblance is far more pronounced, so much so indeed that it can hardly be fortuitous. This possibility of Asiatic influences in Bosch's art is well worth looking into.

From the iconographical angle, the presence of a number of oriental elements in the central panel and left-hand shutter is of no less interest. Circling around the pool—the Fountain of Youth—that forms the focal point of the composition is a cavalcade of figures riding lions, tigers, hyenas, leopards, dromedaries and other animals. On the left-hand shutter an elephant and a giraffe figure on either side of the Fountain of Life, while a palm and another characteristically tropical, cactuslike growth stress the exotic ambience of this delectable vision of the earthly paradise. Here, not for the first time, we come up against a fascinating, if perplexing, question: that of Bosch's sources. What maps, bestiaries or prints can he have consulted? Had he read the *Book of the Wonders of the World* written by Willem de Mandeville between 1407 and 1417 for presentation to the library of the Duke of Burgundy? Then, what of the motifs obviously stemming from Jehan Wauquelin's *Book of the Wonders of India* (1415)? Can he actually have seen the book, or did he get his information at second hand? We do not know, and any attempt to answer these questions would necessitate both diligent research and extreme circumspection.

The composition displays much freedom, combined with disciplined construction. The layout of both the central and left panels is symmetrical; the picture elements are skillfully distributed and balanced, governed by a predetermined rhythm. It is strange indeed that there once was talk of "primitive schematism," a "lack of true co-ordination and cohesion" between the picture elements—showing this to be "a very early work" (Fierens-Gevaert, *Histoire de la Peinture Flamande*, Brussels 1929). Nearly all authorities of Bosch's work—de Tolnay, Combe, Bax, Fraenger, Baldass—concur in regarding this as a perfectly constructed work dating to the painter's prime. This view is confirmed by the underlying significance of the picture as a whole. To grasp this we must do more than merely contemplate its beauties with an appreciative eye. And no sooner do we ask ourselves the question "what does it *mean*?" than we detect a complex symbolism in which each color conveys a message and the whole reveals itself as a highly complex pattern of interlocking, superimposed and overlapping signs. These signs relate to Christian legendry, primitive "analogies," the ethical theories of Ruysbroeck, the secret doctrines of alchemy. Thus pink and red are the colors of love, while all shades of blue signify deceit. Camel, bull, lion and stag are divine symbols. The

The Garden of Earthly Delights: Cylinder with Birds, *detail of the central panel.*

butterfly denotes fickleness, the rat falsehood, the crow unbelief, the monkey lies, the redbreast lust. Cherry and strawberry, grape and pomegranate symbolize sensual delights. The Fountain of Youth, the fabled unicorn, the egg, the crystal globe derive from the arcana of alchemy. The attributes on the heads of the bathing women—crescent, ibis, peacock, etc.—are malefic. A huge owl figures on each side of the garden and there is another inside the globe beneath the Fountain of Life; the owl, Satan's bird, was a familiar symbol of heresy. All the men and women in the *Garden of Earthly Delights* are participating in an orgy, or a daydream, of gratified desires: a sort of cosmic carnival in which plants and animals set the pace. In this grandiose arraignment of the human situation the artist judges and condemns. In the early 17th century Father Joseph Siguenza clearly grasped the purport of this vision of sensual delights and "the triumph of the strawberry," their symbol. "Here we see vivid illustrations of the passages in Scripture relating to man's depravity, for there are many allegories and images in the books of the Prophets and the Psalms that represent it in the form of animals of all kinds, tamed, bold or fierce, slothful and cunning, cruel and carnivorous; draft-animals and steeds used for recreation, pleasure or display, for the gratification of desires and the prestige they give their owners. Here all are represented with remarkable verisimilitude. Would that the whole world were filled with copies of this picture... Men would gain much by contemplating it and then looking into themselves, unless indeed they are so blind as not to see what lurks within them and not to recognize the passions and vices that transform man into an animal, more exactly, a number of animals."

Fraenger, however, has recently challenged the accepted interpretation of this work (*Das tausendjährige Reich*, Coburg 1947). He does not see in the *Garden of Earthly Delights* a message of negation, that is to say an exposure of the sins of the world and a condemnation of the sensual life. On the contrary, the picture, he tells us, indicates the path to follow so as to reach a perfect harmony between the human soul and Nature. According to him it represents Paradise as it was before the Fall and as it will be once again under the rule of the new Adam: the world of the "Millennium," imbued with the divine spirit of love and innocence. Thus the whole picture, Fraenger holds, is an illustration of the rites of a heretical sect to which Bosch belonged, votaries of the "Free Spirit" and addicts of the "cult of Adam." In short, the picture is an exposition of the old, licentious Gnosticism which saw in debauchery a means of spiritual uplift. Fraenger finds in it traces of the "sacred prostitution" sponsored by some eastern religions (see Hutin, *Les Gnostiques*, Paris 1959). It was commissioned, he thinks, by the Grand Master of the Adamites, whom he identifies with the only fully dressed figure (in the bottom right-hand corner of the central panel, at the entrance of the cave of Pythagoras). This man is pointing his index finger at a girl reclining beside him, near a glass cylinder. The seal on her mouth indicates that she is "Guardian of the Secret Knowledge," the new Eve.

Fraenger makes out a persuasive case for his highly original reading of the triptych and there is no questioning his erudition. But it has been vigorously combated, notably by Van Puyvelde, who points out that the author has taken dangerous liberties in his interpretations of the ancient texts he cites. Nor is there any documentary evidence that Bosch belonged to the Adamite sect which flourished in the Low Countries and the Rhineland in the 14th and early 15th centuries (*De Bedoelingen van Bosch*, Amsterdam 1956). In any case the critical spirit so evident in all his work, the high rank he held in the "Swan" confraternity and his relations with the Brothers of the Common Life seem incompatible with membership of a sect of nudist heretics— though he may very well have been acquainted with their doctrines, if indirectly, and been influenced by them up to a point. Finally, we cannot concur with Fraenger's conclusion that Bosch "invented nothing" and confined himself to the role of an executant, the forms, colors and motifs of the picture being prescribed by the Grand Master of the sect of the "Free Spirit." For, to Fraenger's thinking, the merits of the picture are due, in the last analysis, to the praiseworthy docility

The Garden of Earthly Delights, details of the right panel:

◁ The Ladder.

▷ Hanging Demon.

with which he carried out the Grand Master's instructions, and the "Millennium" is a work in which the painter, *qua* painter, played a minor role. But this is tantamount to negating the artist's creative genius, his capacity for inventing images suggested by the theme, his vision and his style. Another major work of Western painting, the Ghent Altarpiece, also conformed to a set program, but who would venture to assert it is more the work of theologians than Van Eyck's? We must not forget that the work of art as such demands initiative, inventiveness, and calls into being a new world obeying no laws but its own. A fact that must be borne in mind particularly in any appraisal of one of the most startling evocations of the diabolic known to painting, the "Musical Hell," third part of the triptych, which we shall continue to call, notwithstanding its grim finale, *The Garden of Earthly Delights*. Here all is chaos, a tangled mass of figures, sinister paraphernalia. The gay colors and the airy freedom harmonizing the left wing (Eden) with the central panel are submerged in clotted darkness, and the logic of sacred reality gives way to the anti-logic of untrammeled fantasy. A new "reality" emerges, the reality of the unreal, product of the autonomous creative imagination, a thorough-going reversal of relations, functions, values, and proportions. In this world of hybrid forms, musical instruments made to hymn God's glory —the harp, the lute, the organistrum and the drum—have become instruments of torture. Even the composition has ceased to be symmetrical, the various episodes are set out in tiers, almost it seems at random, on a bluish ground. All are dominated by the central "tree-man," a pale, fleshless, dessicated, loosely built creature, hardly

The Tree-Man. Drawing.

human at all (the preliminary sketch is in the Albertina, Vienna). His feet are blue boats and his limbs hollow tree-trunks; within his shell-like body (the "world-egg" broken) is a tavern with a flag above it on which figures a bagpipe (in the Vienna sketch there is a crescent, symbol of heresy). A man with the arrow of licentiousness stuck in his back is climbing the ladder leading up to the tavern. Onto the shell is grafted directly a huge human head with an ironical expression on the lips, in which Benesch sees—a tempting hypothesis—a likeness of the painter. Upon the head rests a round, flat disk with a bagpipe on it, providing the music of the Damned. We have already mentioned the alchemical significance of the hollow tree-trunk. Baltrušaitis thinks that this metamorphosis of the tree into a human being derives from an exotic demonology. Be this as it may, the motif, like so many others in the panel, has the stamp of an original creation; indeed, every figure, detail, sign bears the characteristic accent of Bosch's singular genius; is impregnated with the vitality, the charm and visionary sweep distinctive of his art. Line, colors, texture and design—all have that inimitable imprint which is far to seek in certain inferior works that some have sought to attribute to the Bois-le-Duc master.

Bee Skep and Monsters. Drawing.

A *Last Judgment* figures on the central panel of a large triptych now in the Vienna Academy of Fine Arts. Its iconography stems from several sources: the Book of Revelation (upper part); the *Vision of Tondale* (the bridge studded with nails, the slaughterhouse where lecherers are cut in pieces, the cauldron in which murderers are boiled alive, etc.); and the *Shepherds' Calendar* (the gluttons' dinner table, the wheel of torture, and other details). Though the left wing has little to commend it, there are fine pieces of painting, passages of brilliantly handled color, and spectacular foreshortenings in quite the 16th-century manner, in other parts of the triptych. The *gryllus* motif frequently recurs. On the whole, however, this work lacks any clear directive. Indeed there is a piling-up of bizarre details and an exploitation of the grotesque so persistent that it approaches genre painting. This tendency is implemented by the crudity of certain details, the garish colors, the prevalence of dark tones, the somewhat heavy-handed execution and, last but not least, the lack of any truly imaginative drive. Thus we are inclined to see in this overloaded work the imitation of a lost picture: possibly a copy made by Peeter Huys, Bosch's most brilliant disciple.

The Last Judgment, triptych, uncertain dating.

The Last Judgment: Hell, *two details of the right panel.*

The Last Judgment: The Temptress *and* Monster with Basket, *two details of the central panel.*

Fragment of a Last Judgment.

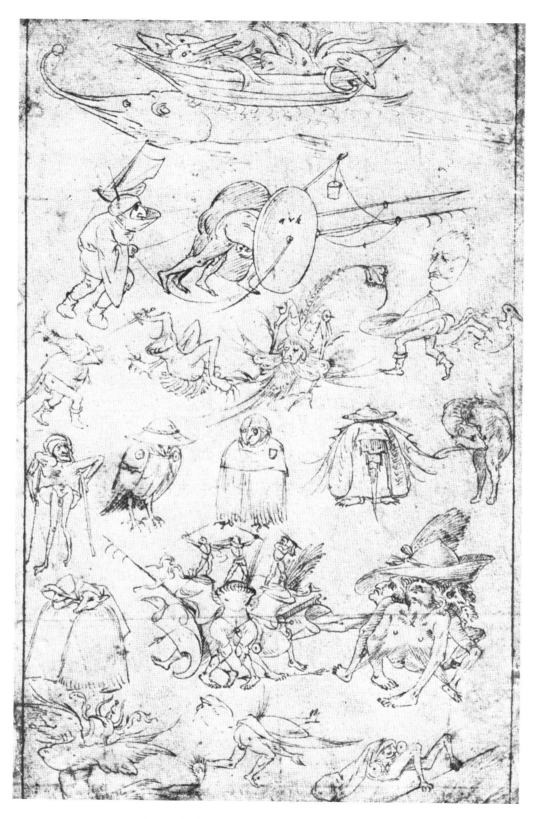

Sheet of sketches with Monsters. Drawing.

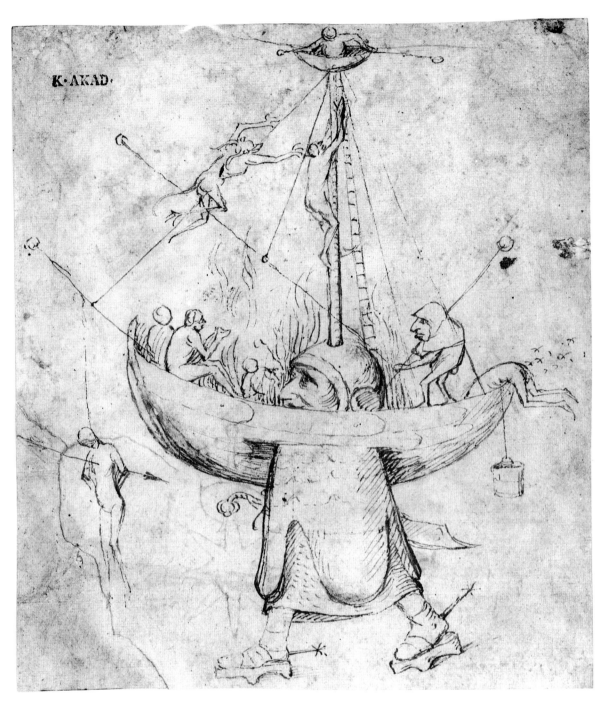

The Demonic Ship Drawing.

The Altarpiece of the Hermits: St Jerome, *central panel, 1505.*

St Jerome in Prayer, about 1505.

THE SHADOWS LIFT

A LOFTY SOLITUDE

The dawn's undoing is the new-born day;
The dusk's is nightfall blanketing the world.
Once there were children of the dawn...
RENÉ CHAR

BETWEEN the tranquil landscape, all in small, light, conventional touches, which acts as a backdrop to the Brussels *Crucifixion* and the luminous, smoothly modulated landscape of the *Temptation of St Anthony* in the Prado, Bosch's art underwent an evolution, one of whose distinctive phases is illustrated by the Ghent *St Jerome in Prayer*. More compact, better composed, less literary than the St Jerome panel in the *Altarpiece of the Hermits* (Ducal Palace, Venice), the Ghent *St Jerome in Prayer* brilliantly combines the poetry of the fantastic and that of nature: nature perverted by Satan and nature in her pristine purity; nature enemy of man and that kindly nature where all is peace, goodwill, serenity.

In the foreground the atmosphere remains polluted. The embers of hell fire still are smoldering and queer little crackling sounds break the silence. The soil is scorched and charred and the vegetation has retained its menacing, jagged spikes. The thorns suggest instruments of torture, the hollow oak recalls a bygone temptation, a broken gourd lies stranded in a pool. Perched on a dead branch, an owl (symbol of

St Jerome in Prayer, detail.

heresy), keeps watch. Colors are warm and forms are skillfully picked out with the luminous white specks characteristic of the Boschian technique. In the midst of this strange setting where all life seems in abeyance, the saint is praying, a crucifix resting on his emaciated arms. He has flung away his scarlet cardinal's robe, it lies across a hollow tree-trunk. In the "holy solitude of the desert, where there are no works of man, no images," he has achieved that "plenitude of bliss" of which Meister Eckhart speaks. There is a striking innovation in the

St Jerome in Prayer, detail.

iconography; hitherto St Jerome had always been depicted fully dressed and kneeling, here he is lying prone, half-naked. (It was left to Jan van Hemessen to strip the saint's figure completely and treat it in the style of the heroic nude.)

The setting is an expanse of open country rendered uniformly in a somber reddish-brown, the foreground spanned by a diagonal that stresses the asymmetry of the composition, articulates the transition between the two planes nearest the beholder, and enables the artist to fill the background with a panoramic vista of hills and meadows. Space is suggested by a bright, sunlit zone, a tract of typically Flemish country rendered in its natural colors, pale, translucent tones of green tinged with ochre. The horizon is set very high and the blue-green of the distant hills, heightening the illusion of depth, anticipates the shimmering effects of "atmospheric" painting.

In this respect *St Jerome in Prayer* has affinities with the Berlin *St John in Patmos*, where an effect of far-flung spatial recession is combined with an atmosphere of profound emotion, a spiritual and plastic purity pervading every element of the scene, and all this is achieved with the utmost simplicity, a fine economy of means. Picture and picture-content are so admirably integrated, the emotive values so closely interwoven with the visual, and all is so perfectly balanced that at first sight one has the impression of a spontaneous creation. Nevertheless, on looking carefully into the work, we see that much thought has gone to its making. It is symmetrically disposed along a central axis, starting from St John's pale face and extending to the church spire on the far horizon. The effect of distance is stressed by the slender tree topped by a thick tuft of leafage just behind the saint. As Fierens-Gevaert has pointed out, Bosch was the first Netherlandish painter to use a tree placed off-center as a spatial referent, determining the scale of the composition. Like the central hill it emphasizes the deep recession of the river scene and meadows bathed in tremulous blue air. The distant townscape, which some have identified with a view of Nijmegen, reminds us of the town that figures in the midst of a desolate plain in the *Cure of Folly* and

St John in Patmos, 1504-1505.

St John in Patmos:
The Angel, *detail.*

also in the background of the *Bearing of the Cross* on the reverse of the right wing of the Lisbon *Temptation of St Anthony*. Also the formal structure of the landscape in *St John in Patmos* resembles that of the panoramic vista on the right wing of the Prado *Adoration of the Magi*. There can be no doubt that all these landscapes point the way to the remarkable developments of Dutch landscape art in the 17th century. In the works we are now considering, frontal presentation is combined with the bird's-eye viewpoint, and we also find an harmonious relation, of both a plastic and a conceptual order, between the human figure and space. Details taken straight from nature are integrated into carefully planned compositions, while the third dimension is suggested by an interplay of values—later to crystallize into the "classical" triad of three planes: brown, green and blue.

This work has several elements of iconographical interest deriving from the Apocalypse. While engaged in writing it, St John is visited by an angel who directs his gaze to "a great wonder in heaven." It is the Virgin "clothed with the sun, and the moon under her feet, and upon her head a crown of twelve stars." In the tree a woodpecker driving away insects symbolizes Christ routing the hosts of Satan. In the distance ships are foundering (Revelation, VIII, 9) and in the foreground the eagle of St John is defying a Satanic monster, half scorpion, half spider (IX, 10), whose human face recalls that of the tree-man,

St John in Patmos:
The Satanic Creature, *detail.*

St John in Patmos: Scenes of the Passion, *reverse.*

central figure in the "Musical Hell" of the *Garden of Earthly Delights*. Bax believes that the prototype of this scene was a miniature in a Dutch manuscript dated 1443 (*Bosschiana, Oud Holland*, 1953), which depicts a small devil taking to his heels and dropping a pitchfork with which he has been trying to seize St John's inkwell. For the saint's face Bosch obviously employed the same model as that of the bridegroom in the *Marriage at Cana*, a fact which may suggest that the two pictures belong to the same period of his career. Moreover, the religious sensibility inspiring both is very similar. However, though the Evangelist's red cloak is still treated in the Gothic manner, this seems a more "advanced" work, later in any case than the *Hay Wagon* with which it is sometimes associated.

On the reverse is a magnificent grisaille. Here fluent execution and masterly brushwork, vibrant, clean-cut drawing, the schematization of visual data and the all-enveloping rhythm recall the stylistic perfection of the outer shutters of the Lisbon *Temptation of St Anthony*. The layout in concentric circles is a return to the archetypal schema employed by Bosch in his first phase, for the *Seven Deadly Sins* (Prado). Seven scenes of the Passion are arranged spoke-wise around a tondo, symbol of the cosmos, floating on a sea of darkness. The bright inner circle, the "eye of God," reflects a rocky island on top of which a pelican is feeding its young with its own blood, symbol of the Redemption. Is it over-fanciful to suggest that this tondo may well owe something to the mandalas of the East, or to some symbolic representation of the Mahometan Kaaba, hub of the universe? (see Berque, *Les Arabes*, Paris 1959.) If so, a Bavarian print made around 1490, representing the Vices and Virtues, may be regarded both as a connecting link between the two works by Bosch we have been comparing and as evidence of the interpenetration of cultures in the period immediately preceding the Renaissance of the North (Baltrušaitis, *op. cit.*).

Quite likely *St John in Patmos* was the right wing of a dismantled triptych. However, we are less inclined to endorse Baldass' theory that the panel *St John the Baptist in the Wilderness* (Museo Lazaro-Galdiano,

St John the Baptist in the Wilderness, 1504-1505.

Madrid) formed the left wing—now reduced in height—of this triptych. In our opinion the two works belong to distinctly different phases of the evolution of the painter's technique and sensibility. Most striking in the first is the subtle play of finely modulated values, in the second, that decorative Gothic bravura which culminated in the *Garden of Earthly Delights*. It belongs, rather, to the Dutch tradition of Geertgen tot Sint Jans, who made a panel treating the same subject. This latter work has been thought to derive from a German print by the anonymous "Master of St John" (see Devoghelaere, in *L'Art et la Vie*, No. 10, Ghent 1936). Assuming that Bosch drew inspiration from the same source, we have here yet another token of his brilliantly creative genius, so vastly has he improved on his "original," and so perfectly has he incorporated in into his highly personal world. In this glorious symphony of reds, dark and light greens, golden yellows, greys and blues, we find a very free interpretation of the Gospel narrative. The wilderness has "blossomed like a rose," the landscape is supremely peaceful, paradisiac, bathed in gentle light, composed (in the exact sense of the word) of meadows, woodlands, cliffs, and distant hills. It reveals a deep feeling for nature and breathes a mood of tranquil meditation implemented by the large recumbent figure in the foreground. Wrapped in a red cloak, resting his arm on a mossy slab, the Baptist is pointing toward the Lamb, emblem of purity, lying in front of a twisted root, symbol of the night side of creation. A characteristically sinister motif marks the transition from reality to the dream: a curious thistle, fleshy, flecked with white and bristling with spines, a growth half plant half reptile. The fruit it bears is poisonous, it is the tree mentioned in the Gospel of St Luke (III, 9) which "bringeth not forth good fruit" and must be cut down. This is confirmed by the dead bird beside it, which has eaten its baneful seeds. The locusts hanging from a branch are a reminder of the Baptist's food in the desert, locusts and wild honey, and the crow perched at the same level signifies unbelief. The huge central sphere, reminder of a leitmotiv of the *Garden of Earthly Delights*, may be intended to represent the fruit of the

The Temptation of St Anthony: The Chapel, *detail.*

mandrake, or perhaps alludes to the occultist practice of placing glass balls in gardens for the purpose of repelling love-charms. Indeed even the pictures which on the face of them seem clearest, most forthright, take on an enigmatic air when we delve beneath the surface for their hidden meanings. For the immemorial strife of good and evil casts its shadow on the background of the artist's thought, however lucid it may seem. And we sense a whole world of sadness, of bleakest pessimism, behind the saint's closed eyes, for even in the desert there is no escaping the awareness of man's corruption.

A small panel seems to us an exception to the rule that it is impossible to establish the chronology of Bosch's oeuvre. This is the *Temptation of St Anthony* in the Prado, at once a departure from hagiographical tradition and unique of its kind in all world art. Here we have the end of a long fever, calm after storm, a lifting of the shadows, the final cadence of a vast and varied tone poem, of the lifelong, fervent proclamation of a message to mankind.

The Temptation of St Anthony: The Monsters, *detail.*

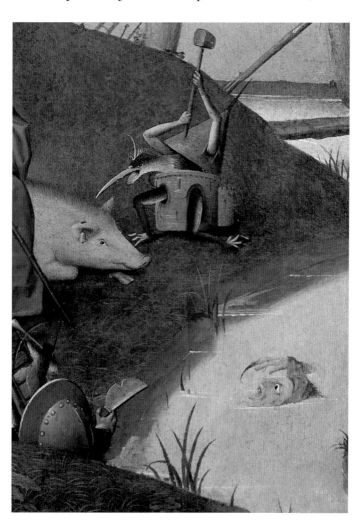

The Temptation of St Anthony, 1504-1505.

Twilight of hell, dawn of a new day—here all is sweetness and light, instinct with silent presences. Moss-green turf, velvety meadows, nature at her kindliest. Slender trees, their crowns of leafage motionless in the still air, measure out space, the shining peace of a friendly countryside, and stress the alternations of clean-cut, highly simplified planes, large zones of green, yellow ochre, blue. The play of verticals and slanting lines, of full and empty spaces, sets the rhythm of a boldly original pictorial construction reflecting the mood of intense concentration that permeates the scene. The aged hermit is seated (not kneeling) in the hollow trunk of a dead tree. His cloak is tightly wrapped around him, his shoulders are hunched and he is resting his head on his clasped hands, rapt in contemplation of an inner vision, letting his gaze "rove the lonely heights" described by Ruysbroeck, "of pure thought stripped clean of images." He is lost in dreams, oblivious to the outside world; nor does he see a helmeted goblin aiming an arrow at him, and another monster on his left, a sort of mobile fortress, with a bird-like head and human hands, crawling up on splayed feet and brandishing a sledge hammer. Nor does he notice Satan's clawed hand reaching up out of the stream in front to beckon him. No longer is he harassed by the temptations of the devil; the peace of the forest has stilled his anguish, his little chapel (of a vaguely oriental type) is undamaged—and overhead the sky is blue.

That morning Bosch laid down his brush. Some importunate visitor had called on him. Echoed by Saint-John Perse, his answer comes to us across the gulf of time:

> Now leave me, I go my way alone.
> I must go out, for I have work in hand,
> An insect's waiting for me, to talk business.

BIBLIOGRAPHY

We have completed the author's bibliography, augmenting the section
"Monographies and Essays" with the most recent publications.

Even today our knowledge of the art of Hieronymus Bosch is largely dependent on the lengthy monograph compiled by Paul Lafond in 1914. Despite its early date, this monograph, which keeps to the analytic, encyclopedic and literary methods of the past, is fully documented, one of its merits being that it constitutes the first inventory of the works of Bosch, of his school and his immediate followers. It enumerates 42 works without any attempt at critical discrimination. It was implemented by the chronological researches made by Baldass (1917, 1938) and Friedländer's stylistic analyses (1927). It is, however, to Charles de Tolnay that we owe the most searching and exhaustive study of Bosch's œuvre (1937). In it de Tolnay not only covered the ground traversed by his predecessors but opened up new paths of research. He inaugurated a critical method of approach involving the concordant use of several disciplines, and drew up the first catalogue raisonné (36 works), based on a close analysis of the master's style and intentions. Baldass followed this up (in 1943 and 1959) in a study largely concerned with the biblical allusions in Bosch's art; Jacques Combe (1946) examined its alchemical sources; Bax (1949) studied its local references and elements of folklore, and Fraenger (in 1947 and 1950) expounded its "heretical" symbolism. Outstanding recent works are the iconographical exegeses published by L. Brand Philip (1953, 1958), C. D. Cuttler (1957) and Fraenger (1957). Finally, we would draw attention to the capital importance of the theories advanced by E. Castelli (1952) and Van Puyvelde (1956).

Within the necessarily limited scope of the present essay, we have tried to situate Bosch's œuvre at the junction of a host of simultaneous influences and trends of thought, but without losing sight of its essential *unity* and, by the same token, of its *quality*, the only sure guide to solving problems of attribution. Thus, we venture to hope, we have helped prepare the way for assigning Hieronymus Bosch his appropriate place in the "history of sensibility" still waiting to be written. Our brief study of this artist's personality would have been more complete could an account have been included of his Protestant convictions and the large part played by the Old Testament in his outlook on life: this would have shown to what extent he may be regarded as a precursor, in the direct line, of both Rembrandt and Van Gogh.
We append a list of the works, some thirty in all, which, in our opinion, can be definitively attributed to Bosch: *The Seven Deadly Sins* (Prado); *The Cure of Folly* (Prado); *The Ship of Fools* (Louvre); *The Man with a Cask* (fragment, Yale University Art Gallery, New Haven); *The Crucifixion* (Brussels); *The Conjurer* (Saint-Germain-en-Laye); *The Marriage at Cana* (Rotterdam); *The Adoration of the Magi* (Philadelphia); *The Hay Wagon* (signed, Prado); *The Bearing of the Cross* (Vienna); *Ecce Homo* (Philadelphia; the Indianapolis version is a copy); *Ecce Homo* (Frankfort); *Death and the Miser* (Private Collection, New York); *The Temptation of St Anthony* (signed, Lisbon); *St Christopher* (signed, Rotterdam); *The Bearing of the Cross* (Escorial); *The Crowning with Thorns* (London); *The Crowning with Thorns* (Escorial); *Christ before Pilate* (Princeton);

Christ Mocked (San Diego); *The Bearing of the Cross* (Ghent); *The Adoration of the Magi* (signed, Prado); *The Garden of Earthly Delights* (Prado); *The Last Judgment* (fragment, Munich); *St Jerome* (Ghent); *St John in Patmos* (signed, Berlin); *The Altarpiece of the Hermits* (signed, Venice); *The Altarpiece of St Julia* (signed, Venice); *St John the Baptist* (Museo Lazaro-Galdiano, Madrid); *The Hawker* (Rotterdam); *The Temptation of St Anthony* (Prado).

Source Books, Documents and Biographical Studies

Rekeningen van de Illustre Lieve-Vrouve Broederschap, Provincial Genootschap van kunsten en wetenschappen in Noord-Brabant, 's-Hertogenbosch (Bois-le-Duc). – *Register der namen en de wapenen der Heeren Beeëdigde Broeders soo geestelijke als wereltlijke van de seer oud en de seer doorlugtige Broederschap van Onse Lieve Vrouw firme de Stad's Hertogenbosch* (idem). – *Lyst van levende en overleden Bruders van 1330 tot 1640* (idem). – *Registres de la Chambre des Comptes de Lille, année 1504*, Archives du Département du Nord, Reg. F. 190. – M. VAN VAERNEWIJCK, *Troubles religieux en Flandre et dans les Pays-Bas au XVIe siècle, 1566-1569* (translated from the Dutch by H. VAN DUYSE and P. BERGMANS, Brussels 1905, p. 137). – G. VASARI, *Le Vite dei più eccellenti Pittori, Scultori e Architettori*, Florence 1568 (English translation by A. B. HINDS, *The Lives of the Painters, Sculptors and Architects*, 4 vols., London 1927). – ARGOTE DE MOLINA, *Libro de la Monteria que mandó escribir Don Alonso, rey de Castilla*, Seville 1582, p. 47. – Fray J. DE SIGUENZA, *Historia de la Orden de San Geronimo, Descripción del Monasterio de San Lorenzo del Escorial*, Madrid 1605, III, pp. 837-841. – L. GUICCIARDINI, *Descrittione di tutti i Paesi Bassi*, Antwerp 1567. – D. LAMPSONIUS, *Pictorum aliquot celebrium Germaniae inferioris Effigies*, Antwerp 1572, No. 3. – G. P. LOMAZZO, *Trattato dell'Arte, Pittura, Scultura e Architettura*, Milan 1585. – C. VAN MANDER, *Het Schilderboek*, Haarlem 1604 (English translation V. VAN DE WALL, *Dutch and Flemish Painters*, New York 1936). – J. B. GRAMAYE, *Taxandria*, Brussels 1610, p. 13. – SANDERUS, *Flandria illustrata*, 1642-1644. – F. PACHECO, *Arte de la Pintura*, Seville 1649, p. 431. – Francisco DE LOS SANTOS, *Descripción breve del monasterio de S. Lorenzo del Escorial*, Madrid 1667. – A. HOUBRAKEN, *De Groote Schouburg der Nederlandsche Kunstschilders en Schilderessen*, Amsterdam 1718. – ORLANDI, *Abecedario pittorico, nel quale sono descritte le vite degli antichissimi pittori, scultori ed architetti, ec accresciuti da P. Guarienti*, Venice 1753. – J. B. DESCAMPS, *La vie des peintres flamands, allemands et hollandais*, Paris 1753-1763. – A. M. ZANETTI, *Descrizione di tutte le pubbliche pitture della città di Venezia*, Venice 1773. – F. DE GUEVARA, *Comentarios de la pintura*, Madrid 1787, pp. 41-44. – J. MORELLI, *Notizie d'opere di disegno scritte da un anonimo*, Bassano 1800. – C. R. HERMANS, *Verzamling van Kronyken, Charters en Oorkonden betrekkelijk de stad en meijerije van 's-Hertogenbosch*, 's-Hertogenbosch 1848. – C. R. HERMANS, *Geschiedenis over den bouw der Sint-Janskerk te 's-Hertogenbosch*, The Hague 1853, p. 13. – A. PINCHART, *Archives des Arts, Sciences et Lettres. Documents inédits*, Ghent 1860, I, pp. 267-278. – Ch. NARREY, *Voyage d'Albert Dürer dans les Pays-Bas*, translated and annotated, Gazette des Beaux-Arts, February 1866, p. 122. – J. C. A. HEZENMANS, *De Illustre Lieve-Vrouwe Broederschap in den Bosch*, Utrecht 1877. – F. XAVIER SMITS, *De Kathedral van 's-Hertogenbosch*, Brussels 1907. – J. DE VORAGINE, *The Golden Legend* (translated by Caxton, 1483). – RUYSBROECK, *Liber de spirituali Tabernaculo*, Groenendael (14th century); *Le Livre du Tabernacle spirituel*, translated by the Benedictines of St Paul in Oosterhout, Brussels 1928-1929. – J. MOSMANS, *De St. Janskerk te 's-Hertogenbosch*, Nieuwe Geschiedenis, 's-Hertogenbosch 1931. – Jean DENUCÉ, *Les galeries d'art à Anvers aux XVIe et XVIIe siècles*, Inventories, Antwerp 1932. – G. MARLIER and J. A. GORIS, *Albert Dürer, Journal de voyage dans les Pays-Bas*, translated and annotated, Brussels 1937, p. 23. – J. MOSMANS, *Jheronimus Anthonis-zoon van Aken alias Hieronymus Bosch, Zijn leven en zijn werk*, 's-Hertogenbosch 1947. -- H.J.M. EBELING, *Jheronimus Bosch*, in *Miscellanea J. Gessler*, Louvain 1948, I, pp. 444-452.

Cultural and Historical Background

ARTEMIDORUS, *Les Jugements astronomiens des Songes*, Troyes 1634. – MALEBRANCHE, N. DE *Recherche de la Vérité*, Paris 1674. – G. SALMON, *Dictionnaire hermétique*, Paris 1695. – PERNETY, *Dictionnaire mytho-hermétique*, Paris 1758. – C.R. HERMANS, *Geschiedenis der Rederijkers in de Noord-Brabant*, 's-Hertogenbosch 1867. – G. ROSKOPF, *Geschichte des Teufels*, Leipzig 1869. – P. LACROIX, *Mœurs, usages et costumes au Moyen Age et à l'époque de la Renaissance*, Paris 1871. – A. GRAF, *La Leggenda del Paradisio terrestre*, Turin 1878. – O. SOMMER, *The Calendar of Shepherds*, London 1892. – Ch. C. VERREYT, *Alart du Hamel of du Hameel, Bouwmeester en Plaatsnijder*, Oud Holland, XII, 1894, pp. 7-10. – A. DE COCK and Is. TEIRLINCK, *Kinderspel en Kinderlust in Zuid-Nederland*, Ghent 1902. – C.F. Xavier SMITS, *De Kathedraal van 's-Hertogenbosch*, Amsterdam-Brussels 1907. – R. VAN BASTELAER and Georges HULIN DE LOO, *P. Bruegel l'Ancien*, Brussels 1907. – E. MÂLE, *L'art religieux de la fin du Moyen Age en France*, Paris 1908. – L. VAN PUYVELDE, *Schilderkunst en Toneelvertoningen op het einde van de Middeleeuwen*, Ghent 1912. – A.W. BYVANCK, *La miniature hollandaise dans les manuscrits des XIVe, XVIe et XVe siècles*, The Hague 1922. – E. PANOFSKY, *Idea*, Schriften der Bibliothek Warburg, Leipzig 1924. – K. KÜNSTLE, *Ikonographie der christlichen Kunst*, Freiburg 1928. – F. LYNA and W. VAN EEGHEM, *Jan van Stijevoorts Refereinenbundel*, Antwerp 1930, pp. 115-117. – E. PANOFSKY, *Hercules am Scheideweg*, Leipzig 1930. – O.A. ERICH, *Die Darstellung des Teufels in der christlichen Kunst*, Berlin 1931. – H. PIRENNE, A. RENAUDOT, E. PERROY, M. HANDELSMAN, L. HALPHEN, *La fin du Moyen Age*, Paris 1931. – J. HUIZINGA, *The Waning of the Middle Ages*, London 1924. – R. VAN MARLE, *Iconographie de l'art profane du Moyen Age et à la Renaissance*, The Hague 1932. – S. FREUD, *Essais de Psychanalyse appliquée*, Paris 1933. – A. MAISON, *Erasme*, Paris 1933. – J. NORDSTRÖM, *Moyen Age et Renaissance, essai critique*, Paris 1933. – Ch. DE TOLNAY, *Pierre Bruegel l'Ancien*, Brussels 1935. – A. PETITJEAN, *Imagination et Réalisation*, Paris 1936. – M. EEMANS, *Les orientations nouvelles de l'art flamand*, Les Beaux-Arts, Brussels, No. 200, 1936, p. 19. – H. PIRENNE, *Histoire de l'Europe, des invasions au XVIe siècle*, Paris 1936. – L. WENCELIUS, *L'esthétique de Calvin*, Paris 1937, p. 401. – R. GRAHAM, *A Picture-Book of the Life of St Anthony the Abbot*, Oxford 1937. – G. JEDLICKA, *Pieter Bruegel. Der Maler in seiner Zeit*, Zurich-Leipzig 1938. – G. BACHELARD, *La Psychanalyse du feu*, Paris 1938. – André LHOTE, *Traité du Paysage*, Paris 1939. – R. GILLES, *Le symbolisme dans l'art religieux*, Paris 1942. – L. FEBVRE, *Le problème de l'incroyance au XVIe siècle*, Paris 1942. – G.K. KERNOLDE, *From Art to Theatre, Form and Convention in the Renaissance*, Chicago 1944. – S. PÉTREMENT, *Le dualisme dans l'histoire de la philosophie et des religions*, Paris 1946. – J.F.A. BEINS, *Misvorming en verbeelding*, Amsterdam 1948. – Gaston BACHELARD, *La terre et les rêveries du repos*, Paris 1948. – André MALRAUX, *Saturne*, Paris 1950, pp. 49-52. – P.R. POST, *De Moderne Devotie. Geert Groote en zijn Stichtingen*, Amsterdam 1950. – Maurizio CALVESI, *Contribution de Gian Paolo Lomazzo à la critique des "Fiamminghi"*, Les Arts Plastiques, 2, 1951, p. 133. – L. DEBAENE, *De Nederlandse Volksboeken*, Antwerp 1951. – Claude ROY, *Goya*, Paris 1952. – A. CHASTEL, *L'Antéchrist à la Renaissance*, Atti del II Congresso internazionale di Studi umanistici, Rome 1952, pp. 177-186. – Mikel DUFRENNE, *Phénoménologie de l'Expérience esthétique*, Paris 1953. – E. GARIN, *Medioevo o Rinascimento*, Bari 1954. – André CHASTEL, *La conscience du cosmos*, in the catalogue of the *L'Europe humaniste* exhibition, Brussels 1954, pp. 27-30. – G. MARLIER, *Erasme et la peinture flamande de son temps*, Damme 1954. – A. GERLO, *Badius Ascencius Stultiferae Naves*, Belgisch Tijdschrift voor Philologie en Geschiedenis, 1954, XXXII, p. 514. – VOLMAT, *L'art psychopathologique*, Paris 1955. – A. KOYRÉ, *Mystiques, spirituels, alchimistes du XVIe siècle allemand*, Paris 1955. – E. PERROY, *Le Moyen Age, Histoire générale des civilisations*, III, Paris 1955. – René HUYGHE, *Dialogue avec le visible*, Paris 1955, p. 320. – Gaston BACHELARD, *La Poétique de l'Espace*, Paris 1957, 2nd edition 1958, p. 120. – J. GRAULS, *Volkstaal en volksleven in het werk van P. Bruegel*, Antwerp-Amsterdam 1957. – G.R. HOCKE, *Die Welt als Labyrinth*, Hamburg 1957. – K. SELIGMANN, *Le Miroir de la*

Magie, Paris 1957. – Jacques Le Goff, Les Intellectuels au moyen-âge, Paris 1957. – Pierre Francastel, Imagination plastique, vision théâtrale et signification humaine, Journal de Psychologie, April-June 1957. – J. Palou, La sorcellerie, Paris 1957. – K. G. Boon, De eerste bloei van de Noord-Nederlandse Kunst, preface of the catalogue of the Middeleeuwse Kunst der Noordelijke Nederlanden exhibition, Amsterdam 1958, pp. 16-31. – Marcelle Bouteiller, Sorciers et jeteurs de sort, Paris 1958. – R. van Luttervelt, De Staatskundige structuur der Noordelijke Nederlanden gedurende de Middeleeuwen, preface of the catalogue of the Middeleeuwse Kunst der Noordelijke Nederlanden exhibition, Amsterdam 1958, pp. 11-15. – M. Caron and S. Hutin, Les Alchimistes, Paris 1959, p. 150. – A. Chastel, Art et humanisme à Florence au temps de Laurent le Magnifique, Paris 1959. – P. Francastel, La sociologie de l'art, La Table ronde, October 1959, No. 142, pp. 9-42. – R. L. Delevoy, Bruegel, Geneva-Paris-New York 1959. – S. Hutin, Les Gnostiques, Paris 1959. – A. and P. Philippot, Le problème de l'intégration des lacunes dans la restauration des peintures, Bulletin de l'Institut Royal du Patrimoine artistique, Brussels 1959, II, pp. 14-15. – H. van Lier, Les Arts de l'espace, Paris 1959. – H. Miller, Big Sur and the Oranges of Hieronymus Bosch, New York 1959. – B. Swain, Fools and Folly during the Middle Ages and the Renaissance, New York, p. 114. – S. Hutin, Histoire mondiale des sociétés secrètes, Paris 1959. – M. Eliade, Les thèmes initiatiques dans les grandes religions, Paris 1959, N.R.F., No. 76, pp. 637-647.

General Works

Since without exception all works dealing with the 16th century or Flemish painting necessarily contain accounts, brief or lengthy, of Hieronymus Bosch, we have thought it superfluous to enumerate here, at the expense of more specialized or less readily available studies of the painter, all those large works covering a wider field which cannot escape the notice of readers interested in our subject.

Monographs and Essays

J. C. A. Hezenmans, Hieronymus van Aken, Dietsche Warande, 1887. – Ed. Geudens, Jeronymus Bosch alias Van Aken, Dietsche Warande, 1890. – C. Justi, Die Werke des Hieronymus Bosch in Spanien, Jahrbuch der Preussischen Kunstsammlungen, X, 1889, pp. 120-144 (republished in Miscellaneen aus drei Jahrhunderten spanischen Kunstlebens, Berlin 1908, II). – M. G. Gossart, Jérôme Bosch, "Le Faiseur de Diables" de Bois-le-Duc, Lille 1907. – L. de Fourcaud, Hieronymus van Aken, dit Jérôme Bosch, Paris 1912. – P. Lafond, Hieronymus Bosch, son art, son influence, ses disciples, Brussels 1914. – L. von Baldass, Die Chronologie der Gemälde des Hieronymus Bosch, Jahrbuch der Preussischen Kunstsammlungen, Berlin 1917, XXXVI, pp. 177-185. – K. Pfister, Hieronymus Bosch, Potsdam 1922. – W. Schurmeyer, Hieronymus Bosch, Munich 1923. – L. Baldass, Betrachtungen zum Werke des Hieronymus Bosch, Jahrbuch der kunsthistorischen Sammlungen in Wien, 1926, pp. 103-118. – M. J. Friedländer, Geertgen van Haarlem und Hieronymus Bosch. Die Altniederländische Malerei, V, Berlin 1927. – A. M. Hammacher, Jeroen Bosch, Vrije Bladen 1936. – Ch. de Tolnay, Hieronymus Bosch, Basle 1937. – L. Baldass, Zur künstlerischen Entwicklung des Hieronymus Bosch, Annuaire des Musées Royaux des Beaux-Arts, Brussels 1938, pp. 47-71. – M. Brion, Bosch, Paris 1938. – W. Gaunt, A Fifteenth Century Surrealist: J. Bosch, The Studio, 1938. – A. Hals, Die Rätsel der Bilder von Jeroen Bosch, Munich 1938. – F. M. Huebner, Hieronymus Bosch, Berlin 1939. – A. Vermeylen, Jeroen Bosch, Amsterdam 1939. – M. J. Friedländer, Hieronymus Bosch, The Hague 1941. – F. M. Huebner, Jeroen Bosch als Mensch en Kunstenaar, The Hague 1942. – F. M. Huebner, Jérôme Bosch, Brussels 1943. – L. von Baldass, Hieronymus Bosch, Vienna 1943 (2nd edition, 1959). – X. de Salas, El Bosco en la Literatura Española, Barcelona 1943. – L. van den Bossche, Jeroen Bosch, Diest 1944. – J. Combe, Jérôme Bosch, Paris 1946 (2nd edition, 1957). – J. de Bosschère, Jérôme Bosch, Brussels 1947. – Howard Daniel, Hieronymus Bosch, Paris 1947. – W. Fraenger, Hieronymus Bosch. Das Tausend-

jährige Reich. Grundzüge einer Auslegung, Coburg 1947. – J. V. L. BRANS, *El Bosco en el Prado y en el Escorial*, Barcelona 1948. – D. BAX, *Ontcijfering van Jeroen Bosch*, The Hague 1949. – J. LEYMARIE, *Jérôme Bosch*, Paris 1949. – A. BERTRAM, *Jerome Bosch*, London 1950. – W. FRAENGER, *Die Hochzeit zu Kana. Ein Dokument semitischer Gnosis bei Hieronymus Bosch*, Berlin 1950. – W. FRAENGER, *Der Tisch der Weisheit, bisher "Die sieben Todsünden" genannt*, Psyche, Stuttgart 1951. – W. VOGELSANG, *Hieronymus Bosch*, Amsterdam 1951. – G. DORFLES, *Bosch*, Milan 1954. – G. VAN CAMP, *Autonomie de Jérôme Bosch et récentes interprétations de ses œuvres*, Bulletin des Musées Royaux des Beaux-Arts 3, Brussels 1954, pp. 131-148. – L. BRAND-PHILIP, *Hieronymus Bosch*, New York 1955. – W. HIRSCH, *Hieronymus Bosch, "The Garden of Delights,"* London 1955. – J. R. TEXEIRA LETE, *J. Bosch*, Rio 1956. – L. VAN PUYVELDE, *De Bedoelingen van Bosch. Lezing gehouden op 10 October 1955 in de vergadering van de afdeling Letterkunde der koninklijke Nederlandse Akademie van Wetenschappen*, Amsterdam 1956. – O. BENESCH, *Hieronymus Bosch and the Thinking of the Late Middle Ages*, Konsthistorisk Tidskrift, Stockholm 1957. – Cl. A. WERTHEIM-AYMES, *Hieronymus Bosch*, Amsterdam 1957. – W. VOGELSANG, *Hieronymus Bosch*, Amsterdam 1958. – W. FRAENGER, *The Millennium of Hieronymus Bosch*, Chicago 1951, London 1952. – C. LINFERT, *Hieronymus Bosch, The Paintings*, London 1959. – Cl. A. WERTHEIM-AYMES, *Die Bildersprache des Hieronymus Bosch*, The Hague 1961. – J. DE BOSSCHÈRE, *Jérôme Bosch et le fantastique*, Paris 1962. – M. GAUFFRETEAU-SÉVY, *Jérôme Bosch*, Paris 1965. – F. M. HUEBNER, *Le mystère Jérôme Bosch*, Brussels 1965. – I. MATEO-GOMEZ, *El Bosco en España*, Madrid, Consejo superior de Investigaciones Científicas 1965. – M. BUSSAGLI, *Bosch*, Florence 1966. – M. J. FRIEDLÄNDER, *Tout l'Œuvre peint de Jérôme Bosch*, Paris 1967. – M. POCH-KALOUS, *Hieronymus Bosch in der Gemäldegalerie der Akademie der Bildenden Künste in Wien*, Vienna 1967. – Ch. DE TOLNAY, *Jérôme Bosch* (descriptive catalogue), Paris 1967. – P. REUTERSWÄRD, *Hieronymus Bosch*, Stockholm 1970. – F. M. HUEBNER, *Jérôme Bosch*, Brussels 1971. – C. LINFERT, *Jérôme Bosch*, Paris 1972. – R. H. MARIJNISSEN, K. BLOCKX, P. GERLACH, *Hieronymus Bosch*, Brussels 1972. – SYLVESTRE, *Essai d'interprétation du triptyque du* Char de foin *de Jérôme Bosch*, Dijon 1973. – Ch. VAN BEUNINGEN, *The Complete Drawings of Hieronymus Bosch*, London 1974. – J. E. MÜLLER, *Bosch*, Paris 1976. – J. P. JOUFFROY, Le Jardin des délices *de Jérôme Bosch grandeur nature*, Paris 1977. Cl. METTRA, *Jérôme Bosch*, Paris 1977. – G. MARTIN, *Jérôme Bosch*, Paris 1978. – J. ROWLANDS, *Hieronymus Bosch:* The Garden of Earthly Delights, Oxford 1979. – COLL., *Hieronymus Bosch: Die Rezeption seiner Kunst im frühen 16. Jahrhundert*, Berlin 1980. – L. S. DIXON, *Alchemical Imagery in Bosch's Garden of Delights*, Ann Arbor, Michigan 1981. – D. HAMMER-TUGENDHAT, *Hieronymus Bosch, eine historische Interpretation seiner Gestaltungsprinzipien*, Munich 1981. – Ch. DE TOLNAY, *Jérôme Bosch*, Paris 1984. – A. D'ACHON, *Jérôme Bosch: par-delà l'envers et l'endroit*, Paris 1984. – W. BOSING, *Hieronymus Bosch c. 1450-1516: between Heaven and Hell*, Cologne 1987. – M. BUSSAGLI, *Bosch*, Florence 1988. – H. HOLLÄNDER, *Hieronymus Bosch: Weltbilder und Traumwerk*, Cologne 1988. – C. LINFERT, *Jérôme Bosch*, Paris 1988. – R. H. MARIJNISSEN, *Hieronymus Bosch: Das vollständige Werk*, Weinheim 1988.

Specialized Studies

The Fantastic in Bosch's Art:

L. MAETERLINCK, *Le genre satirique dans la peinture flamande*, Brussels 1907. – L. MAETERLINCK, *Le genre satirique, fantastique et licencieux dans la sculpture flamande et wallonne*, Paris 1910. – E. J. HASLINGHUIS, *De duivel in het Drama der Middeleeuwen*, Leiden 1912. – C. VETH, *Geschiedenis van de Nederlandsche caricatuur en van de scherts in de Nederlandsche beeldende kunst*, Leiden 1921. – A. CHASTEL, *La tentation de saint Antoine ou le songe du Mélancolique*, Gazette des Beaux-Arts, XV, 1936, pp. 218-229. – C. ROGER-MARX, *Les Tentations de saint Antoine*, La Renaissance, Paris, March-April 1936, pp. 3-22. – G. MARLIER, *Les visions démoniaques de Jérôme Bosch et de ses émules*, Le Soir,

Brussels, February 18, 1941, p. 10. – P. FIERENS, *Le Fantastique dans l'art flamand*, Brussels 1947. – E. LANGTON, *La démonologie, Etude de la doctrine juive et chrétienne*, Paris 1951. – E. CASTELLI, *Il Demoniaco nell'arte. Il significato filosofico del demoniaco nell'arte*, Milan 1952, pp. 62-76; French translation, *Le Démoniaque dans l'art*, Paris 1958, pp. 21-26, 67-71. – C. LINFERT, *Die Vermummung, eine Figuration der Angst und der Lüge in Bildern von Bosch, Bruegel und Max Beckmann*, Cristianesimo e Ragione di Stato, Atti del II Congresso di Studi umanistici, Rome 1952. – C. R. PICCINATO, *Il significato divino dell'arte demoniaca dei pittori nordici dei secoli XV e XVI*, Cristianesimo e Ragione di Stato, Atti del II Congresso di Studi umanistici, Rome 1952. – H. SEDLMAYR, *Art du démoniaque et démonie de l'art*, Arch. Filosofia, 1953, I, pp. 99-114. – P. FIERENS, *La tradition du fantastique en Belgique*, Les Arts Plastiques, June 1954, pp. 5-20. – F. NEUGASS, *Das Phantastische in der Kunst*, Kunstwerk, 1954, No. 6, pp. 4-26. – J. BALTRUŠAITIS, *Le Moyen-âge fantastique*, Paris 1955, pp. 42-46. – J. BALTRUŠAITIS, *Le paysage fantastique au moyen-âge*, L'Œil, No. 10, 1955, pp. 18-22. – W. FRAENGER, *Die Versuchung des hl. Antonius von H. Bosch*, Archivio di Filosofia, Padua 1957. – C. D. CUTTLER, *Witchcraft in a work by Bosch*, The Art Quarterly, XX, 2, 1957. – C. D. CUTTLER, *The Lisbon Temptation of St Anthony by Jerome Bosch*, The Art Bulletin, XXXIX, 2, 1957. – E. VON PETERSDORFF, *Dämonologie*, Munich 1957-1958. – R. CAILLOIS, *Anthologie du Fantastique*, Paris 1958. – F. HELLENS, *Documents secrets*, Paris 1958. – J. STERNBERG, *Une introduction au fantastique*, L'Observateur, Paris, October 9, 1958, pp. 15-16. – A. MASSON, *Le Jardin des Délices*, Critique, No. 144, 1959, pp. 427-432. – L. VAX, *L'art de faire peur*, Critique, No. 150, 1959, pp. 915-942; ibid., 151, 1959, pp. 1026-1048. – C. ROY, *Psychologie du fantastique*, Les Temps modernes, 1960, No. 167-168, pp. 1393-1416.

Interpretation of Proverbs:

F. GOEDTHALS, *Les proverbes anciens flamengs et françois correspondans de sentence les uns aux autres*, Plantin, Antwerp 1568. – G. J. MEYER, *Oude Nederlandsche spreuken en spreekwoorden*, Groningen 1836. – C. TUINMAN, *De Oorsprong en uitlegging van dagelijks Gebruikte Nederduitsche Spreekwoorden*, Middelburg 1726-1727. – H. HOFFMANN, *Niederländische Sprüchwörter, Denksprücher und sprüchwörtliche Redensarten*, Breslau 1838. – P. J. HARREBOMÉE, *Spreekwoordenboek der Nederlandsche Taal*, Utrecht 1858-1870. – K. J. WANDER, *Deutsches Sprichwörter-Lexikon*, Leipzig 1867-1880. – P. H. VAN MOERKERTEN, *De satire in de Nederlandsche Kunst der middeleeuwen*, Amsterdam 1904. – A. DE COCK, *Spreekwoorden en zegswijzen afkomstig van de oude gebruiken en volkszeden*, Ghent 1905. – SEILER, *Deutsche Sprichwortkunde*, Munich 1922. – F. A. STOETT, *Nederlandsche spreekwoorden, spreekwijzen, uitdrukkingen en gezeden naar hun oorsprong en beteekenis verklaard*, Zutphen 1923-1925. – D. ROGGEN, *Het verklaren van het werk van Bosch en Bruegel*, Nieuws Vlanderen, No. 10, March 7, 1936.

Miscellaneous:

H. DOLLMAYR, *Hieronymus Bosch und die Darstellung der vier Letzten Dinge in der niederländischen Malerei des XV. und XVI. Jahrhunderts*, Jahrbuch der kunsthistorischen Sammlungen des Allerhöchsten Kaiserhauses, Vienna 1898, XIX, pp. 284-310. – L. MAETERLINCK, *Une œuvre inconnue de Jérôme Bosch*, Gazette des Beaux-Arts, 1900, pp. 68-74. – A. MAROUAND, *A Painting by Hieronymus Bosch in the Princeton Art Museum*, Princeton University Bulletin, XIV, 1903, pp. 41-47. – G. GLÜCK, *Zu einem Bilde von H. Bosch in der Figdor'schen Sammlung in Wien*, Jahrbuch der Preussischen Kunstsammlungen, Berlin 1904, XXV, p. 174 (republished in *Aus drei Jahrhunderten europäischer Malerei*, Vienna 1933). – L. MAETERLINCK, *A propos d'une œuvre de Bosch au Musée de Gand*, Revue de l'art ancien et moderne, 1906, XX, pp. 299-307. – F. SCHMIDT-DEGENER, *Un tableau de Jérôme Bosch au Musée Municipal de Saint-Germain-en-Laye*, Gazette des Beaux-Arts, 1906, I, pp. 147-154. – L. TRAMOYERES BLASCO, *Un Triptico de Jeronimo Bosco en el Museo de Valencia*, Archivo de Arte Valenciano, 1915, I, pp. 87-102. –

L. DEMONTS, *Deux primitifs néerlandais au Musée du Louvre*, Gazette des Beaux-Arts, 1919, pp. 1-20. – FIERENS-GEVAERT, Introduction to the Catalogue of the *Flemish Landscape Exhibition*, Brussels 1926, pp. 7-8. – H. F. W. JELTES, *Een Hieronymus Bosch in het Rijksmuseum*, Elseviers Geïllustreerd Maandschrift, Rotterdam, 1927, LXXIV, p. 75. – W. VOGELSANG, *Een vroeger Navolger van Hieronymus Bosch*, in *Mélanges Hulin de Loo*, Brussels 1931, pp. 333-337. – Otto BENESCH, *Ein Spätwerk von Hieronymus Bosch*, in *Mélanges Hulin de Loo*, Brussels 1931, pp. 36-44. – W. EPHRON, *Hieronymus Bosch. Zwei Kreuztragungen*, Vienna 1931. – D. HANNEMA, *De Verloren Zoon van Jheronymus Bosch*, Jaarverslag Museum Boymans, Rotterdam 1931, pp. 2-5. – G. GLÜCK, *Die Darstellung des Karnevals und der Fasten von Bosch und Bruegel*, in *Gedenkboek A. Vermeylen*, Antwerp 1932, pp. 263-268. – H. MEIGE, *L'opération des pierres dans la tête*, Aesculape, 1932, XXII, pp. 50-62. – D. Th. ENKLAAR, *De Blauwe Schuyt*, Tijdschrift voor Geschiedenis, 1933, pp. 37-64, 145-161. – E. BUCHNER, *Ein Werk des Hieronymus Bosch in der älteren Pinakothek*, Münchner Jahrbuch der Bildenden Kunst, XI, 1934. – L. BALDASS, *Ein Kreuzigungsaltar von H. Bosch*, Jahrbuch der kunsthistorischen Sammlung, Vienna 1935, p. 87 ff. – M. FLORISOONE, *J. Bosch et les primitifs néerlandais à Rotterdam*, L'Amour de l'Art, 1936, p. 302. – W. SCHÖNE, *Die Versuchung des heiligen Antonius. Ein wenig bekanntes Bild im Escorial*, Jahrbuch der Preussischen Kunstsammlungen, 1936, pp. 57-64. – H. DEVOGHELAERE, *Le Saint Jean-Baptiste de la collection J. Lazaro*, L'Art et la Vie, Ghent 1936, 10, pp. 312-318. – L. BALDASS, *Die Zeichnung im Schaffen des H. Bosch und der Frühholländer*, Graphische Künste, 1937, II, p. 156. – O. BENESCH, *Der Wald, der sieht und hört*, Jahrbuch der Preussischen Kunstsammlungen, LVIII, Berlin 1937. – H. DEVOGHELAERE, *Interprétations de la Nef des Fous de Jérôme Bosch*, L'Art et la Vie, Ghent 1937, 2, pp. 43-50. – J. DUPONT, *Le retable Saint Antoine du Musée national de Lisbonne*, Brussels 1937. – J. KNUTTEL, *Hieronymus Bosch en de tegennatuurlijke dingen*, De Gids, 1937, II, p. 64. – E. D'ORS, *Hieronymus Bosch*, Almanach des Arts, Paris 1937, pp. 235-239. – J. DESTRÉE, *Jérôme Bosch*, Bulletin de l'Académie Royale des Sciences, des Lettres et des Beaux-Arts de Belgique, Brussels 1938, p. 138. – *A Great Jerome Bosch for San Diego: "Christ taken in Captivity,"* Arts News, December 1938, p. 6. – J. GRAULS, *Taalkundige toelichting bij het Hooi en den Hooiwagen*, Gentsche Bijdragen tot de Kunstgeschiedenis, Antwerp 1938, V, pp. 156-175. – P. FIERENS, *Jérôme Bosch et les "Préhollandais,"* Le Journal des Débats, Paris, September 1, 1938. – E. G. A. GALAMA, *Twee zestiende-eeuwse spelen van de Verlooren Zoon door Robert Lawet*, Utrecht 1941. – J. G. VAN GELDER, *Teekeningen van Jeroen Bosch*, Beeldende Kunst, No. 8, 1941. – L. LEBEER, *Het Hooi en de Hooiwagen in de beeldende Kunsten, De Ets "Al Hoy,"* Gentsche Bijdragen tot de Kunstgeschiedenis, Antwerp 1938, V, pp. 152-155. – Ch. DE TOLNAY, *A Temptation of St Anthony by Hieronymus Bosch*, Art in America, 1944, p. 61. – J. COMBE, *Jérôme Bosch dans l'art de Bruegel*, Les Arts Plastiques, 11-12, 1948, pp. 435-446. – W. FRAENGER, *Hieronymus Bosch; Johannes der Täufer*, Zeitschrift für Kunst, 1948, pp. 163-175. – Ch. DE TOLNAY, *An Early Dutch Panel: A Contribution to the Panel Painting before Bosch*, in *Miscellanea Leo van Puyvelde*, Brussels 1949, pp. 49-54. – Lauro VENTURI, *Les Films sur l'art en Italie*, Les Arts Plastiques, Brussels 1949, 1-2, pp. 34-35. – G. VAN CAMP, *Considérations sur le paysage de Jérôme Bosch*, in *Miscellanea Leo van Puyvelde*, Brussels 1949, pp. 65-73. – W. FRAENGER *Johannes auf Patmos. Eine Umwendtafel für den Meditationsgebrauch*, Zeitschrift für Religions- und Geistesgeschichte, II, 1949-1950, pp. 327-345. – G. RING, *Hieronymus Bosch*, Burlington Magazine, January 1950, p. 28. – A. PIGLER, *Astrology and Jerome Bosch*, Burlington Magazine, May 1950. – G. CHABOT, *Le Musée des Beaux-Arts de Gand*, Brussels 1951, p. 14. – W. FRAENGER, *Hieronymus Bosch in seiner Auseinandersetzung mit dem Unbewussten*, Du, Schweizerische Monatsschrift, 10, 1951. – H. SCHWARZENSKI, *The Battle between Carnival and Lent*, Bulletin of the Museum of Fine Arts, Boston 1951, 275, pp. 10-11. – C. JANSON, *Le "Christ en Croix" de Jérôme Bosch*, Bulletin des Musées royaux des Beaux-Arts, I, Brussels 1952, pp. 83-88. – A. E. POPHAM, *An Unknown Drawing by Hieronymus Bosch*, Actes du XVIIᵉ Congrès International d'Histoire de l'Art, Amsterdam 1952, pp. 247-250. – L. BALDASS, *La tendenza moralizzante in Bosch e Bruegel*, Atti del II Congresso Internazionale di Studi Umanistici, Rome 1952. – W. FRAENGER, *Hieronymus Bosch, Der verlorene Sohn*, Cristianesimo e Ragione di Stato, Rome 1952. – J. V. L. BRANS, *Un nouveau Bosch au Musée du Prado*, Gazette des Beaux-Arts, 40, 1952, pp. 129-131. – D. BAX, *Bosschiana, Verloren Zoon, Johannes op Patmos, Wellusttuin, Doornenkroning*, Oud Holland, 1953, 68, pp. 200-208. – L. BRAND-PHILIP, *The Prado Epiphany by Jerome Bosch*, The Art Bulletin XXXV, No. 4, 1953, pp. 267-293. – W. FRAENGER, *Il "Figliol prodigo" di Hieronymus Bosch*, Arch. Filosofia, 1953, I, pp. 127-136. – K. SELIGMANN, *Hieronymus Bosch, The Pedlar*, Gazette des Beaux-Arts, 1953, 42, pp. 97-104. – H. SCHUMANN, *Hieronymus Bosch "Paradies der Liebe,"* Kosmos v. Ekklesia, 1953, pp. 77-83. – A. VIEIRA SANTO, *Hieronymus Bosch. As Tentações de Santos Antão do Museu Nacional de Arte antiga de Lisboa*, Lisbon 1953. – W. VAN BESELAERE, *Het Kerstthema by Bosch en Bruegel*, Westflanderen, 3, 1954, pp. 8-15. – J. DION, *Le "Concert dans l'œuf" de Bosch*, Amis du Musée de Lille, 1954, No. 12, pp. 11-12. – L. VAN PUYVELDE, *De Geest van Hieronymus Bosch*, Revue belge d'Archéologie et d'Histoire de l'Art, 1954, p. 238. – M. WALICKI, *Hieronima Boscha dialog ze światem*, Prz. artyst., 1954, No. 5-6, pp. 101-116. – J. V. L. BRANS, *Los Ermitanos de Jeronimo Bosco, San Juan Bautista en el Desierto*, Goya, 4, Madrid 1955, pp. 196-201. – M. SALAZAR, *El Bosco y Ambrosio de Morales*, Archivo Español de Arte, 1955, 28, pp. 117-138. – L. SERVOLINI, *Gusto di Jheronimus Bosch*, Arte figur. ant. mod., 1955, No. 1, pp. 30-31. – H. SCHWARZENSKI, *An Unknown Bosch*, Bulletin of the Museum of Fine Arts, Boston 1955, 53, pp. 2-10. – G. VAN CAMP, *Une Tentation de saint Antoine à rattacher à l'œuvre de Jérôme Bosch*, Revue belge d'Archéologie et d'Histoire de l'Art, 24, 1955, pp. 29-38. – D. BAX, *Beschrijving en poging tot verklaring van het Tuin der Unkuisheiddrieluik van Jeroen Bosch*, Amsterdam 1956. – W. FRAENGER, *Die Versuchung des Hl. Antonius von H. Bosch*, Archivio di Filosofia, Padua 1957. – *Une restauration extraordinaire: Le Portement de Croix de Jérôme Bosch*, Connaissance des Arts, 63, 1957, pp. 50-53. – L. BRAND-PHILIP, *The Pedlar by Hieronymus Bosch. A study in detection*, Nederlandsche Kunst Jaarboek, 1958. – L. LEBEER, *Frans Hogenberg, Al Hoy*, Trésors de la Bibliothèque Royale de Belgique, 1958, pp. 134-137. – *Révélation au Musée des Beaux-Arts de Gand, un chef-d'œuvre retrouve son vrai visage*, Connaissance des Arts, 71, 1958, pp. 36-37. – R. VAN SCHOUTE, *Le Portement de croix de Jérôme Bosch au Musée de Gand. Considérations sur l'exécution picturale*, Bulletin de l'Institut Royal du Patrimoine artistique, Brussels 1959, II, pp. 47-58. – Catalogue of the *La Miniature flamande* exhibition. *Le Mécénat de Philippe le Bon*, Brussels 1959, pp. 23 and 87.

LIST OF ILLUSTRATIONS

(Unless otherwise specified, all illustrations are from archive photographs)

PRINTED BY
IRL IMPRIMERIES RÉUNIES LAUSANNE S.A.
BOUND BY
MAYER ET SOUTTER S.A., RENENS-LAUSANNE

Printed in Switzerland